PLANNING
and
HUMAN SURVIVAL

PLANNING
and
HUMAN SURVIVAL

Melville C. Branch

PRAEGER

New York
Westport, Connecticut
London

Library of Congress Cataloging-in-Publication Data

Branch, Melville Campbell, 1913–
    Planning and human survival / Melville C. Branch.
        p.   cm.
    Includes bibliographical references and index.
    ISBN 0–275–93826–3 (alk. paper)
    1. Social policy.   2. Planning.   3. Human ecology.   I. Title.
HN28.B73   1992
    361.6′1—dc20   91–44569

British Library Cataloguing in Publication Data is available.

Library of Congress Catalog Card Number: 91–44569
ISBN: 0–275–93826–3

First published in 1992

Praeger Publishers, One Madison Avenue, New York, NY 10010
An imprint of Greenwood Publishing Group, Inc.

Printed in the United States of America

The paper used in this book complies with the Permanent
Paper Standard issued by the National Information Standards
Organization (Z39.48–1984).

10 9 8 7 6 5 4 3 2 1

Appreciation is expressed to my wife,
Hilda S. Rollman-Branch, M.D.
Both the content and language of this book
have benefited from her thorough and
perceptive review of the manuscript.

Consisting of a single nucleic acid and surrounded by a protein coat, a virus is the simplest form of life. It is also the only other organism on earth, besides ourselves, capable of threatening human survival.

Thomas A. Bass,
Camping with the Prince and Other Tables of Science in Africa (1990)

CONTENTS

INTRODUCTION

The author's last four books, including this one, represent a progressively broader examination of planning. *Comprehensive City Planning: Introduction and Explanation* (1985) explains that city planning is the product of actions by many organizations, the two most important being the planning performed by the legislative body and operating departments of the municipality and the land-use activities of city planning commissions and departments.

Regional Planning: Introduction and Explanation (1988) describes this activity as conducted by civil governments, businesses, and the military services. These different applications have been treated separately and regarded as distinct, academically and in practice, although they employ the same basic process of planning in different ways for different particular purposes.

Planning: Universal Process (1990) presents planning as a process inherent in the individual actions and collective activities of people. It is rooted in the billions of years during which animate life evolved on earth from the simplest cellular beginnings. It has existed as a conscious and deliberate endeavor in humanoids for several hundred thousand years and advanced dramatically during the past ten thousand years of human civilization.

During this period different kinds of planning have developed with common procedural characteristics, and the process has been institutionalized in different societies as an established way of thinking and acting. A core of knowledge and certain recognized procedures have been identified as fundamental to its effective application. There have been great successes and great failures, but the remarkable advance of civilized society during an infinitesimal fraction of evolutionary time demonstrates that people can plan constructively.

At the same time, man has created problems that not only affect his prospects on earth but also threaten his survival as a species. They are treated in this book without the reluctance of too many people to ac-knowledge disturbing realities and the refusal of many decision makers to consider existing problems as they really are and incorporate them in planning analysis and action.

Evolutionary forces that advanced animate life during billions of years can no longer direct human development by themselves. We now have the capability as a species of animal to affect the planet and ourselves by our numbers and our technological achievements to such an extent that we are a global force determining together with nature the future of life on earth.

The march of civilization has placed people on the path of self-determination whether we like it or not, whether we can handle it or not. We cannot depend on a benevolent nature, evolution, fortunate mutation, or beneficial random chance to somehow ensure a successful future for our species.

The condition and prospects of people depend on planning more than any other of their activities, within the overarching effects of global nature and the surrounding universe. It is our only hope of coping, surviving, and improving our condition—unless we are willing to accept nature's possible correction of our unplanned, often thoughtless, and destructive actions: overpopulation, pollution, the rapid exhaustion of irreplaceable natural resources.

Our misbehavior could be curtailed for us by new diseases that reduce the human population until it no longer threatens the balance of nature. ''Even if you could impose the perfect program for screening international travellers, infected people will get in, and some of your own citizens will come back infected. . . . And how confident are we that another previously undiscovered virus isn't today having its own silent phase of spreading throughout the world.''[1] Or nature may find another way of restricting our transgressions.

Drastic alterations of natural conditions brought about by nuclear war, destruction of the protective ozone layer, or significant greenhouse warm-ing of the earth's atmosphere and climatic change could decimate or eliminate the human species. Human society could self-destruct if defi-ciencies of food and shelter; disparities between haves and have-nots; racial, tribal, and religious animosities; or crime, violence, and localized armed conflict become intolerable. Or it could be forced into a form of rigid organization, control, and compartmentalization of its members sim-ilar to those developed in nature to ensure the survival of some animal societies, or the type of robotic society postulated by George Orwell in *1984*.

Faced with the degree of self-determination we have achieved, will we act to attain the best future we can for ourselves within the environment of earth, ocean, and atmosphere in which we exist? We know that planning is an inherent aspect of everything we do. It is intrinsic even in our unconscious motor reactions. We plan all the time: intuitively, automatically, and with conscious and deliberate forethought. We are aware that we can intentionally direct our actions over a period of time to produce impressive accomplishments of many kinds. We recognize that our capability to produce desired results can be applied for good or evil, for individual or collective purposes, for public or private interests, for specific objectives as diverse as the scope of human activities and desires.

The crucial question at this point in time is, Can we apply planning to progressively advance ourselves as individuals and as a society, and favor our survival as a species? This means functioning with careful regard for the limitations imposed and opportunities presented by our environment that we can neither escape nor transcend. It requires actions that are mutually supportive rather than isolated, overcompetitive, or conflictive. It requires looking ahead and acting with reference to the longer-range future as well as the immediate present. Waiting until conditions become so threatening that the necessity of remedial action finally is acknowledged does not produce optimum results. It can produce breakdown or catastrophe.

This book extends the author's inquiry into planning by examining man's capability to carry it out effectively. Does man have or can he acquire the qualities required? Or is the handwriting already on the wall for his societal disintegration or disappearance as a species in the distant future? What are the critical problems he faces? Do human characteristics favor successful planning? What social conditions affect planning for the longer-range future? How do the mass media relate to planning? What substantive content and procedural features of the planning process itself are required for its effective application? What types of planning are involved? And, finally, what signs or measures will indicate whether planning is successful in advancing the human prospect?

Although civilization has produced the accumulation of knowledge required to plan and carry out the myriad projects and activities completed by man, little has been recorded concerning the process of planning itself and the specific applications that made these achievements possible. Almost nothing has been written describing the basic process that underlies the widespread employment of planning: selection and treatment of the information needed, the analysis required, optimum ways of reaching conclusions, making decisions, implementing plans, monitoring and learning from the results.

In the same way that abstract mathematics is the foundation for the many derivative forms and applications of mathematical knowledge, identifying the fundamentals of the planning process will provide the basis for improvement in its many applications: most importantly at the highest level of political and managerial decision making where it is most needed and least applied.

Successful planning is the critical requirement for human survival— barring a major celestial collision or a geological convulsion within the planet that wipes out Homo sapiens. "We can surely destroy ourselves, and take many other species with us, but we can barely dent bacterial diversity and will surely not remove many millions of species of insects and mites. On geological scales, our planet will take good care of itself and let time clear the impact of any human malfeasance."[2]

The author has attempted to make this book easy to read by avoiding professional jargon, technical terms, and excessive citations supporting every statement of fact or judgment. His observations and conclusions are derived from more than fifty years' experience and study of urban, regional, and corporate planning and matters relating to these activities.

REFERENCES

1. Bass, Thomas A., "A Hero in the War on AIDS," *Harvard Magazine*, November-December 1990, pp. 63, 65.
2. Gould, Steven Jay, "The Golden Rule—a Proper Scale for Our Environmental Crisis," *Natural History*, September 1990, p. 30.

Part I

THE EXISTING
SITUATION

CRITICAL PROBLEMS CONFRONTING HUMAN SOCIETY

There is more doubt and uncertainty now than at any other time in recent history: doubt in our political process and in our priorities; skepticism with respect both to intelligent and rational thought and to the contribution of science and technology; and serious doubt about commitment to honesty and justice. All of this is exacerbated by the positive feedback of opinion polls, by staged televised pronouncements, and by economic uncertainties that are more severe than we have known since the Great Depression—uncertainties that result from a total absence of planning. There is a lack of confidence in leadership. At the same time, there is the urge to be led, which is always manifest when there is a crisis of major import.

Leonard M. Rieser
Science (April 1974)

The world is beset today with problems that in their magnitude and diversity exceed anything faced by human society in the past. Undoubtedly, early humanoids and primitive people were confronted at times with environmental conditions that threatened their survival. But the multiple problems facing the five and a quarter billion people on earth today constitute a universal threat comparable in its destructive potential to the unknown event that extinguished the dinosaurs—the predominant animal species 66 million years ago.

Most people are concerned primarily with their own needs and desires, and those of their family. They become aware of a societal problem when it affects them immediately, directly, and personally—or when it is treated repeatedly on television or in a newspaper they view or read regularly.

They have no need or motivation to consider societal problems as a whole, to become acquainted with their collective impact.

Also, most people consciously or unconsciously avoid thinking about problems that are latent rather than immediate, especially those whose effects are indirect, will not have their full impact until some future time, and are not fully understood. Who wants to bear in mind continually emotionally disheartening and disturbing difficulties? Particularly if we believe that we are powerless as individuals to do anything about it even when we are motivated to take action. For some people, too much attention paid to problems precludes retaining the hope that makes life worthwhile and—however unrealistic or misguided—gives confidence that somehow critical problems will disappear or resolve themselves without serious consequences in the meantime. For others, divine faith requires accepting whatever problems arise, with confidence that they will be taken care of by supernatural intervention. "There's a divinity that shapes our ends, Rough-hew them how we will."[1] In addition to the difficulties of acknowledging critical societal problems, most of them are also complex and hard to understand. Few people will study them sufficiently to judge their importance and formulate a sound judgment concerning what should be done.

Since planning is the only hope of resolving or at least mitigating crucial problems, the political leaders of society must take them to heart. Programs of remedial action must be instigated before crises develop, even if the population at large neither comprehends nor cares. We can no longer depend on evolutionary nature to gradually resolve man-made problems without constructive actions on our part. Without this combination of natural forces and human actions, we will slowly but surely disintegrate and ultimately disappear as a species.

The primary problems are different among countries and at different times, depending on the geographical, social, and economic nature of the country, its stage of technological development, its history and culture, or some other determinative factor. In a poverty-stricken land in the first stage of its societal development, the major problem and need is likely to be feeding an expanding population with food produced internally rather than imported, requiring payment by barter or in a foreign currency, and creating a basic dependency on another country. Critical problems in nations with advanced economies and technology are likely to involve automated industries, complex operational systems, and sophisticated products characteristic of scientifically and technically mature societies.

The primary problems of some societies reflect particular characteristics or conditions. In a nation with deep and pervasive religious beliefs and culture, preserving the faith and maintaining the role of religion are primary objectives of planning in the eyes of the populace and its leaders. Military preparedness is a continuing requirement for a nation in a militarily strategic location with hostile neighbors it has fought repeatedly in the past. Nations with international ambitions dependent on military power require more than a defensive military establishment. Long-lasting national hostilities, religious conflicts, ethnic rivalries, autocratic conditions, or the lingering effects of historical events can dominate planning and exclude consideration of critical needs. Planning in a nation with its economy and public institutions captive to the illicit production and distribution of drugs reflects this exceptional situation.

Customs and attitudes can discourage or preclude people acknowledging the existence or the importance of major difficulties. Or for one reason or another and in one way or another, politics or governmental bureaucracies can see to it that the public is not even aware of certain critical problems, much less sufficiently informed concerning them to demand remedial action. "For 14 years [a British epidemiologist] battled a policy of scientific secrecy that she said threatened the lives of thousands of workers in weapons plants and of people living near them . . . prompting a Congressional committee to investigate allegations of a scientific cover-up."[2]

Although the problems facing human society are diverse, as noted briefly in the previous paragraphs, those discussed on the following pages are universally significant. They do not all apply, of course, to every country at all times. But they represent areas of societal importance, concern, and need that have existed in every country at some time in its past, exist today, or will exist at some time in its future. To the extent these problems can be categorized as latent rather than existing, the human condition is vastly improved and the existence on earth of the human species is greatly extended.

WAR, ARMED CONFLICT

Nuclear war is recognized by most people as the foremost catastrophic threat. For years the United States and Soviet Union have had the capability of obliterating each other with land-based and submarine-launched ballistic missiles with multiple-targeted nuclear warheads. Nuclear weapons also are carried by aircraft and cruise missiles, and artillery shells can incorporate nuclear explosives.

Although the global extent and duration of the "nuclear winter" following all-out atomic war still are debated, few people doubt that radioactive contamination affecting most forms of animate life would extend far beyond the areas totally obliterated by direct explosive impact and lethally poisoned by radioactivity. Radioactive fallout from the Chernobyl nuclear accident was borne by prevailing winds halfway around the world.

Elimination of the nuclear stand-off between the United States and the late Soviet Union leads some people to conclude that nuclear war cannot occur. Although reduced tensions between the superpower nations have lessened the possibility of nuclear war on a global scale, they have not eliminated it. The capability of the United States and Russia to destroy each other still exists, and is unlikely to be eliminated for some time to come.

History has demonstrated time and again that the availability of military might is important in the inevitable competition and conflict between nations during peacetime. Many more nations will have operational nuclear missiles by the turn of the century. This increases the possibility—if not the probability—of "localized" nuclear wars and the danger of attempts by demented heads of state to surreptitiously trigger a nuclear war between other nations. The spread of atomic capability will be the ultimate outcome of widespread sale of military weapons around the world—a recognized part of many nations' manufacture of products for export and profit, or conducted clandestinely by "merchants of death."

> The spread of strategic weapons to unstable regions greatly increases the likelihood that they will be used. We cannot reverse the process and so must learn to manage its consequences. Ballistic missiles and other means of long-range destruction, traditionally limited to a handful of industrialized nations, are fast becoming a fixture in many regional conflicts . . . political, economic, and technological factors have produced an array of nations that can deliver conventional, nuclear, or chemical warheads.[3]

The military presence is still very much a part of civilization, requiring higher- and higher-priced weapons as they become more sophisticated and lethal. There is general agreement that military expenditures could be applied to greater human advantage for civil needs. But the prospect of nuclear war or the use of chemical or biological weapons has not diminished as a primary problem confronting humanity as a whole. Any lessening of the danger of global nuclear war between the superpowers is offset by the increasing likelihood of nuclear conflict between smaller nations at a regional level, triggered by tribal, territorial, religious, or other strong differences. Hostile groups occupy particular areas within a state, extend across national boundaries, or exist as a minority or majority of the population in many countries around the world. Past events, different faiths or customs, and identification with particular territories create antagonisms and active opposition in daily life that can escalate into armed conflict. At all times nowadays in at least a dozen countries, there are armed hostilities between neighboring nations, opposing groups within a nation, or revolutionary insurrections.

CRIME, TERRORISM, VIOLENCE

The proliferation of weapons and their widespread availability are certainly related to the increases in crime that are disrupting society in many parts of the world. Crime has isolated and physically devastated large areas of some cities and made them unsafe for most people and ordinary activities. It has expanded beyond individual criminal acts, to organized crime directing large-scale production and distribution of drugs, prostitution, extortion, illegal business, financial fraud, and money laundering. As human activities become more diverse and technically complex, crime follows suit in its continuing challenge to the established mores and legal activities of individuals and societies.

Local terrorism by gangsters, mobs, and other dissident groups has expanded to international terrorism against groups of people, global transportation and communication systems, even entire populations. It has become commonplace and never-ending in some countries: 335 reported terrorist attacks and 6,231 episodes of intimidation in one nation of some 35 million people during one month in 1990. In another country, a report on conditions after ten years of civil war tells of "boys as young as 8 years old turned into killers, of 10-year-old girls raped repeatedly, of children forced to witness or even participate in the murder of their parents. Thousands of people have reportedly been massacred, hundreds of villages destroyed, families torn apart."[4]

The violence associated with crime and terrorism in its more extreme form has been a more benign element in the evolution of human beings since their early origin, in connection with hunting to obtain food, protecting the family, and guarding the territory required to support a community from attack by other animals and hostile humans. These defensive antagonisms have developed all too often during ten thousand years of civilization into wanton and deliberate cruelty: genocide, mass murder, atrocities carried out against individuals. Reports in daily newspapers and television news broadcasts refute any doubt that violence is widespread and accelerating throughout the world today.

> Alarmed by violence in the parks . . . the [U.S.] National Park Service has urged all rangers to wear bulletproof vests . . . crime is now a problem throughout the park system, long prized as a sanctuary from the worst of urban and suburban life. [In the first six months of 1989] rangers and drug agents have seized more than $500 million in narcotics from national parks.[5]

It is seen in more and more ordinary activities: among spectators at athletic events who indulge in partisan violence; in the conduct of some sports that are becoming almost gladiatorial contests; in movies and television programs; and in some fraternal, religious, and extremist groups incorporating cruelty in their rituals. Different cultures view violence differently. For some it has been part of acceptable and even desirable human sacrifice. But certain acts are considered violent by almost everyone: cruel treatment and murder of innocent bystanders and hostages, mutilation, and hurtful overreaction far in excess of what is justified by the provocation.

The behavioral restraints of civilized society are fragile. All too often they are disregarded by individuals in fulfilling a personal desire, acting on the spur of the moment, or yielding to the ever-present temptation of illicit activity. Or large numbers of people collectively abandon established restraints by looting, rioting, or otherwise acting in ways normally impermissible if not unthinkable. Obviously, terrorism and violence threaten the stability of civilized society. When populations outgrow the capacity of a nation to maintain existing living standards, the pressure for violent reaction increases. And societies are more vulnerable to disruption as human activities become more complex and subject to technical malfunction, and a large proportion of their population lives in cities where they are almost totally dependent on other people for vital services. Such destabilizing conditions make constructive planning all the more difficult.

ADDICTION

Different people around the world have used small amounts of drugs for centuries to counter the debilitating effects of living at high altitudes, to provide moderate stimulation, or to obtain the pleasurable psychic effects of various substances. These uses have not been progressively addictive, nor have they gotten out of societal control sufficiently to alter the traditional moral and socioeconomic systems of the countries involved.

Drugs are a primary problem in parts of the world. In the United States, the growing number of drug users and dealers can threaten the established order, political system, and social welfare of the nation. Addicts steal and assault people to satisfy their dependence on drugs. Drug traffickers commit murder and mayhem in connection with the many criminal transactions in which they are engaged. Hundreds of thousands of people are illegally financing, producing, transporting, distributing, and selling drugs. Juveniles and children are enlisted or forced to participate. As a consequence of illegal drug activities, crime and violence are increasing in the United States. "Homicide rates have continued to soar [in 1990], and experts attribute the rise to an increase in drug disputes, deadlier weapons and a tendency among more young people to start careers in crime with a gun."[6] Drug addiction severely damages the health of users, making them less productive members of society requiring a disproportionate share of public services. Many children of addicted parents are born with physical abnormalities that shorten their life expectancy or damage them in some way for the rest of their lives.

The costs of drug control are enormous: a burden on the individual taxpayer, an unproductive element of the national economy, and a disruptive force in societal affairs. The vast sums of money derived from illegal traffic in drugs are spent on personal consumption, to bribe law enforcement and judicial officials, to purchase legitimate businesses, and to generally increase the illicit activities and corruptive power of the criminal elements of society. The relation between drug traffic and poverty, low income, and unemployment add to the difficulties of drug control. For many drug dealers on the streets, this may be their only and certainly their most lucrative source of income. For some it means the difference between hunger and nourishment as long as they believe no alternative exists. Active "employment" in drugs is preferable to standing all day on a street corner with nothing to do, or engaging in some other less-profitable illicit activity.

To slow the flow of drugs by reducing their production at the source abroad, instead of reducing demand in the afflicted country, means asking nations producing large quantities of drugs for export to forego a significant percentage of their gross national product. Besides the drug manufacturers losing their source of income, those engaged in the countryside growing the plants from which the drugs are derived could no longer support themselves and their families in this way. Many of them would join the ranks of the unemployed. The national economy and political stability would be weakened. In countries where drug barons have accumulated such wealth and power that they are in fact the sovereign government, the problem of reducing drug production at the source is far more difficult and may prove impossible.

Alcohol is second only to drugs in its destructive effects on millions of individuals in the United States, their families, and society as a whole. These include all the effects described above for drugs, but their relative impacts are somewhat different and less severe. Tobacco, of course, is the third major addiction, reduced in recent years by laws restricting its use in public places and announcements on products disclosing its harmful effects.

POVERTY, HUNGER, DISPARITIES

The Bible confirms that with very few exceptions "the poor always ye have with you." When the human population was a fraction of what it is today after a century of almost exponential growth, the poor were far fewer in number, a smaller proportion of the total, and not as different from most of the population. Today, some 30 million people in the United States are officially classified as below the "poverty line." At least a quarter of the world population lives in poverty as a distinct "underclass," too poor to obtain enough food to maintain health and perform a job. They suffer the severe privations of the poor: inadequate food and shelter, little or no money income, unhealthful environmental conditions, no education, no health care, and little prospect for a better future for themselves or their children.

For these reasons the poor comprise the least economically productive segment of society, alienated by their privations, lack of formal education, higher unemployment, and standards of behavior suited to the harsher realities of their existence compared with other people. Many live in dilapidated neighborhoods, squatter settlements, or as homeless on the streets of large cities where they have come hoping to improve their condition. In parts of the developing world the rural poor remain bound to economically depressed or environmentally devastated countrysides where abject poverty can lead to famine, starvation, and death.

A few societies with smaller populations have largely eliminated poverty because of exceptionally favorable economic conditions, such as Saudi Arabia and Brunei with the enormous wealth derived from their oil fields. Others such as Sweden and Denmark have adopted social policies of economic subsidy and other forms of support for the poor. But most nations are not able or do not elect to eliminate poverty. Few human societies are committed to taking care of all their members.

The population explosion in recent years has increased the number and comparative percentage of poor people in the world, particularly in developing countries where growth has been the greatest. And with their higher birthrates, the poor continue to multiply at a faster rate than the rest of the population. The disparity between the haves and the have-nots also continues to widen. The accumulation of great fortunes and financial power by relatively few people today is reminiscent of past epochs when the wealth of royalty and an elite aristocracy dominated the peasantry and the poor. In the United States, top executive salaries, stock options, bonuses, "golden parachutes," and special consultant and retirement arrangements reflect special privilege more than rewards for performance above and beyond that expected of top management. The number of multimillionaires in the United States has multiplied three times in less than ten years to a grand total of 260,000.

Young people under age 16 now constitute a third of the world population and probably an even larger percentage of the poor. Television enables them to see clearly the disparities between their lot in life and the wealth, material possessions, societal advantages of the well-to-do. They appear on television as the principal participants in civil disturbances around the world. And as indicated in the previous section on addiction, many of them are engaged in drug traffic and other criminal activity as the only way they know of making a living. The potential for destructive social conflict is high. As President François Mitterrand of France summarized the situation:

> There is madness in not striving to reduce the gap between the rich and the poor. This gap is more dangerous than nuclear bombs. When people do not

have enough to eat, and this will soon be the case of eight out of ten human beings, their revolt can prove impossible to check. Developed countries have to be very attentive to the plight of poor countries.[7]

HOUSING DEFICIENCIES

Shelter takes many different forms in different environments, depending on the climate, culture, customs, and the economic and political situation of the society. But all shelter serves three basic purposes: to provide protection from the weather, to retain heat within the structure, and provide privacy or separation from immediate surroundings. Inadequate housing is implicit in the classification of several billion people in the world today as poor, although some of them in less-developed parts of the world are content with the typical shelter to which people in the community are accustomed: huts and houses constructed with local materials, without any of the utilities and amenities associated with dwellings in industrialized societies. As civilization progresses, however, the hopes of the poor rise to match advances in the standard of living, and aspirations are kindled to attain some of the features of modern homes seen on television, in magazines, and in newspapers.

The clearest evidence of global housing needs are the squatter settlements in large cities in many countries: Mexico City, Rio de Janeiro, Sao Paulo, Manila, Hong Kong, Kuala Lumpur, Istanbul, Lagos, or the sidewalks of Calcutta. They are ringed or dotted with such settlements: jerrybuilt of discarded or purloined materials on illegally occupied land—the only kind of shelter available for millions of people who have migrated from depressed rural areas to cities in the hope of a better life. One-half of Mexico City's 16 million inhabitants and over a quarter of the entire population of South America are reported to live in squatter settlements, devoid of municipal utilities, services, and restraints. Rural housing is equally inadequate in many parts of the world, except that the availability of local building materials and more open space make living with poverty less onerous. Keeping up with population growth imposes a continuing need for new shelter that must be met by more squatter settlements or additional conventional housing.

The United States must not only house its increasing population and replace structures when they are no longer usable, but single-parent households double the need for dwelling units for this growing segment of society. Foreign workers in nations accepting them require a place to live where they are employed and earning money to send back home to their families. The building industry in the United States is capable of physically producing all the housing needed, included dwellings that low-income and poor people can afford. However, there are many reasons why this is not done, which are vigorously debated by the actors and interest groups involved: high costs of construction and land, difficulties of financing, a lengthening list of desired features in dwelling units, governmental restrictions and requirements, bureaucratic delays, competing demands on available funds, unwillingness of many governments to provide subsidies.

As is the case with providing sustenance for the poor noted in the previous section, neither the federal government nor any of the states have a clear-cut policy and program of actions to adequately house the economically disadvantaged. Although various efforts are made to subsidize housing for lower-income people, reliance is still placed in the United States on the marketplace to produce the needed housing by the "trickle down" or gradual amortization and deterioration of older apartments and houses until they are affordable for those with low incomes. In effect, providing housing for the poor has been ignored in the United States, until it has become impossible recently to disregard the homeless wandering on the streets during the day and sleeping near the exhaust grilles of the heating systems in large buildings at night. The advance of civilization or of a nation could well be judged by its willingness and capability to provide adequate sustenance for its most disadvantaged members and to support programs that gradually reduce their numbers.

EDUCATIONAL DEFICIENCIES

There can be little doubt that education is of extreme importance in human existence and societal advance. The process of transmitting information for survival and betterment, and its accumulation over time as a store of knowledge, begins with learning from one's parents and the surrounding environment, followed by successive levels of formalized education. Educational needs depend, of course, on the existing and perceived situation. Primitive people need a critical body of knowledge to survive and prosper. In rudimentary societies this is acquired, collected, and transmitted verbally from person to person. The accumulation of knowledge needed in industrially and technologically advanced societies is much greater because the elements of civilized existence are more numerous and complex. Written words and symbols in books, computer memories, and other means of storing information comprise the necessary core of knowledge. More education is required to make a living and otherwise participate successfully in modern society. As human knowledge expands and deepens, individuals can retain a smaller and smaller fraction of what is relevant to their needs and objectives. Coordination of specialized knowledge and collaborative investigation become ever more essential.

Especially in industrialized nations with democratic governments, a minimum "general education" is necessary to understand the issues presented for public reaction, to participate constructively as a citizen, formulate sound political judgments, and vote intelligently on crucial matters increasingly difficult to understand. To this base of comprehension must be added the particular knowledge needed to succeed in one of the myriad occupations ranging from manual labor to the most sophisticated professions. While most people agree with these generalizations, there is great disagreement concerning the content of the needed knowledge: between those of different age groups, income levels, ethnic backgrounds, religious beliefs, or established customs, and between different government systems. There are almost as many specific prescriptions as there are different people and points of view. This is why there is periodic controversy in the United States concerning the selection of high school textbooks, involving state legislators, local school boards, faculties, and parent-teacher associations. Society's decision concerning the content and diversity of its educational system is probably the most important determinant of its future path and prospects.

In the world today, trade and transportation, financial affairs, and instant communication interconnect all parts of the world. This interaction and interdependence call for similar knowledge on the part of more and more people in more and more countries. In the meantime, the poor and disadvantaged need at least a minimal formal education to improve their lot as individuals and participate in the advancement of their society. The preponderant "middle class" also requires the level of formal education needed to keep pace with an increasingly technical and complicated world.

Of the hundreds of millions of people around the world who are illiterate, 20 million are employees in the U.S. work force. Another 20 million or more Americans are not well enough educated to perform successfully in a world with more and more of its activities requiring at the very least the equivalent of a high school education. But the way many high school students are performing today, this may not be enough unless standards are raised. More than one-half of high school students cannot explain economic terms that are commonly employed in commercial, governmental, and international affairs. Reports indicate that American students generally are deficient in writing, geography, science, mathematics, and foreign languages. "We abuse mathematics by failing to apply even the little we know of it to the false or questionable ideas that we encounter. We do not want to be duped, but most of us are fooled on a regular basis by politicians, the media and even friends."[8] With such educational deficiencies it is next to impossible to function in a world in which greater knowledge, global interaction, and international competition are facts of life. Immigrants need to learn the native language of their new homeland if they are to participate fully in its activities rather than remain linguistically different and culturally isolated.

Not enough students are graduating in scientific and engineering specializations to meet the needs of industries and service organizations in the United States. The number of young people dropping out of high schools or not attending school at all is especially alarming among several minority groups. This contributes to unemployment, broken families, crime, delinquency, and discontent. Those so disadvantaged by lack of education are among the have-nots who are most prone to social resentment, angry reaction, and civil disturbance.

PUBLIC HEALTH

The poor are most afflicted by sickness because of malnutrition, unsanitary living conditions, and little or no health care. In tropical countries with average per capita incomes of less than U.S. $400 a year, nearly one person in ten suffers from a disease. Chief among these, affecting some 600 million people, are malaria, schistosomiasis, onchocerciasis, and lymphatic filariasis causing elephantiasis. The prevalence of such diseases increases as the exploitation of natural resources damages the environment, and as civil unrest dislocates people and in other ways increases the stresses and strains of everyday life. Large segments of the population of some economically distressed or politically turbulent nations are forced to migrate to escape famine or violence.

Worldwide diseases threaten large numbers of people. Most of the world population was infected by the influenza epidemic after World War I. Twenty-five million people died, more than the total casualties of the conflict. New strains of flu emerge frequently and require new vaccines. No one knows how many casualties will result from the acquired immune deficiency syndrome (AIDS). It is estimated that by the year 2000, 30 million people will be infected with this disease. Populations have been decimated in the past by the introduction of new diseases against which there is no natural or rapidly acquired resistance. "Less than fifty years after Cortez landed, the population of central Mexico had been reduced to about one-tenth of the size it [was] before contact."[9] Today, the spread of infectious organisms, previously localized, is facilitated by the great increase in personal air travel and the shipment of goods among all regions of the world.

Urbanization, industrialization, and technological developments are introducing new health hazards. Overburdened sanitary systems and toxic waste sites cause bacteriological infection and chemical poisoning. Operations at nuclear plants generating electricity and producing atomic weapons can cause radiological sickness and organic bodily damage when safety provisions are inadequate, and sudden death if there is an accidental discharge of radioactive material. The explosion in 1986 of a nuclear reactor at the Chernobyl electric generating plant near the Baltic Sea in what is now the independent Ukraine exposed 600,000 people to the harmful effects of airborne radioactive fallout. The exposure of people around plutonium manufacturing plants and atomic weapons test sites in the United States is just now being revealed by the federal government and evaluated by all concerned. Studies suggest that there may be injurious effects from electromagnetic radiation generated by high-voltage electric transmission installations, certain industrial and office equipment, and some household appliances. And new carcinogenic substances are being identified it seems almost every day.

The sicknesses, diseases, and injuries confronting Homo sapiens constitute the problem of protecting the public health—a task so diverse and widespread in industrialized countries that individuals, groups, and organizations must voluntarily comply with preventive and curative measures established in the public interest. No nation can afford the huge army of inspectors that would be required to continually monitor and enforce every activity subject to the many laws, regulations, and requirements needed to safeguard the public health.

THE FAMILY UNIT

In prehistoric times, the family was the unit of evolutionary survival. Its members were fed and sheltered, the young taught by parents and elders, and the family protected from outside harm to the extent possible. It has continued as the basic operating unit of society, a major force shaping its current activities and its future. In most societies the family entity includes the immediate family consisting of parents, children, grandparents, and grandchildren, and an extended family of more distant relatives, which may include a few or many additional people. Families give their members an emotional identification and attachment that is crucial for the healthy development of the child and an important support for the adult. They reduce social isolation. They provide assistance in time of need and a sense of security that greatly eases the personal burdens of everyday living. They transmit attitudes, customs, and beliefs to succeeding generations. Not all families exhibit these positive attributes. Not only do aberrations occur in families, but there has been at least one primitive society in which normal family behavior was almost totally absent, with individual self-interest and extreme personal selfishness governing every action.

For the billions of people living in rural areas around the world, the family is still the critical socioeconomic unit. And in cities where more and more people are congregating, it is the most important unit of cohesion among individuals and the basic building block of societal development. In the United States, however, disturbing changes are occurring in the characteristics and behavior of families when they are split in two by divorce and separation. The discord that caused the break-up often escalates into hostility between parents and further emotional disturbance for the children. There is no father figure in the household of the single mother living alone with the children. Since the mother probably must seek employment because of the difficulties of enforcing child support awards against the father, day care becomes a problem for the mother and another emotional adjustment for the children.

The number of split families is increasing rapidly in the United States. In one state one-half of all marriages end in divorce or separation. Besides the disruption this causes within the family noted above, there are other repercussions. The housing market is affected because additional dwelling units must be built to house the single parent who no longer lives at home. Divorce cases further burden an overloaded judicial system; few benefit economically besides the lawyers. More and more families today are unwilling to care for elderly parents within the family home. This is even likelier to be the case with broken families. For those who can afford it, some provision for elderly parents outside the family home is the preferred solution. "The rise in numbers of single parents, unmarried couples, and people living alone isn't unique to the U.S. A Bureau of Labor Statistics study found that these situations are common to most countries in the developed world. The difference is in the pace at which these trends are progressing."[10]

Other factors are affecting families more generally. In poor households there is the temptation for the young to engage in drug trafficking for profit. They may find membership in a gang more supportive and satisfying than their own family, which may be riven by hostilities. Or adult members may have conflicting views concerning permissible behavior by younger members of the family. As life expectancies increase, the age difference between the young and the elderly increases, intensifying attitudinal differences and lengthening the time during which elderly parents may be a burden in or outside the home. Increase in the number of two-income families usually results in less parental time and attention for the family in the home. And in modern societies fewer and fewer of the elements of survival and prosperity are related to the family as an entity rather than to its members separately.

To the extent that such divisive developments continue in the United States and occur elsewhere in the world, the historical role and functioning of the family unit is affected. "The number of women [in the United States] who have never married and are rearing children as their own has increased sharply.... In 1987 there were 2.6 million women who had never married rearing children under 21 years old whose fathers were not living in the home."[11] Certainly, the stabilizing influence of the family unit in society is being reduced, eliminating a source of economic support and security for the individual, and generally increasing crime, delinquency, high school drop-outs, and disregard for law and order. A number of the social functions performed within the family may be gradually transferred to government, some other social organization, or perhaps ignored with unknown consequences.

RELIGION

Religious beliefs probably originated when humans first became consciously aware of the awesome forces of nature: violent storms with thunder and lightning, earthquakes and volcanoes, hurricanes and tornadoes. It was natural that early humans considered these frightening and threatening events as expressions of an all-powerful force or god. Belief that worshipful acts could propitiate the gods was the next step in the development of religious faith and ritual practice. Over thousands of years this early beginning developed into religions as we know them today. During this period they have been responsible for or involved in major wars and countless local conflicts, and also in what are considered today as great cruelties: crucifixion, human sacrifice, burning at the stake, torture, and imprisonment—considered at the time proper acts by the blessed against heretics. Any attitude or almost any act was justified or called for in the name of one's own god.

Concurrently, religions have produced religious art, architecture, and music. They have formulated their respective precepts and codes of moral behavior, one of the bases for our civil systems of law and order. Throughout this development there was the range of strict observance, partial conformance and nonconformance, proper behavior and misbehavior characteristic of all collective human activities. Religious and civilized behavior evolved in concert. To effectively administer operations involving many people and activities far and wide, the major religions have contributed to the development of forms of organization employed in human endeavors. Some have successive levels of hierarchical control extending from divine interpretation and decision at the top, to intermediate levels of regional direction, to local administration and monitoring. Other forms of religious organization involve collegial decisions and activities.

The outstanding feature of religions as a group is their diversity. They vary in size and scope from many million members located in numerous countries around the world to a few hundred in a single locality. The particular divinity and the rituals of worship differ enormously. The age of formal religions extends from only 30 years to over 3,000 years. Some are very politically active, in some nations the dominant force in the government. Some have accumulated great monetary wealth and extensive physical possessions. Certain religious faiths are fixed in their beliefs and militant in their actions; others are tolerant and permissive.

Diversity notwithstanding, there are common characteristics among religions. They are in general agreement that a divinity directs human destiny and there is some form of continuation after death. They are dynamic, seeking more members and greater spiritual and societal influence. Religious revelation, inspiration, and decision are considered by believers superior to any form of civil determination. Although the nature and depth of religious commitment varies greatly among individuals, most people have some religious identification or belief in some kind of universal force. Emotions are not only the most vital element in human behavior, they are dominant in religious beliefs since scientific rationality can play almost no part in confirming the divine. As a consequence of their common characteristics, religions constitute a primary force in human affairs and a major factor in the progress of civilized society—the most powerful force in many situations at times, and in some countries predominant for prolonged periods. Religions present fewer difficulties for society in themselves than the fact that they always pose the important question: How should they relate to secular society as it becomes more complex, technical, and environmentally sensitive?

MATERIALISM

Material possessions have become the primary objective of more and more people in countries with strong enough economies to provide the disposable income or credit needed. Television, newspapers, and other mass media carry advertising, news reports, and stories to all parts of the world, calling the attention of hundreds of millions of people to a vast array of products. It is the primary purpose of many enterprises to attract as many people as possible to the cornucopia of material things that exist for those who can afford them. The have-nots are repeatedly made aware of what others have that they do not. This is not conducive to individual and societal contentment and political stability. Witness the indiscriminate looting that occurs in many places when there is an electrical power blackout or some catastrophic event weakens normal property protection.

Materialism can create a constructive motivation for people to work harder to acquire more possessions, or envy, resentment, and discontent on the part of the have-nots. It can result from or lead to an "ethical doctrine that consideration of material well-being, especially of the individual himself, should rule in the determination of conduct."[12] This is the antithesis of religious doctrine that emphasizes the importance of spiritual values for the individual, to the extent that in some religions a total absence of worldly goods is the mark of special piety and an obligation for others to sustain the mendicant.

There are broad social effects that result from strong emphasis on material possessions. Materialism accentuates the here and now, things that can be attained and enjoyed during one's lifetime rather than at some future time benefitting someone else. People are apt to judge each other on the basis of what they possess rather than their qualities as individuals. These consequences are especially disturbing in the young.

> Young Americans have become far more materialistic and far less idealistic since the mid-1970s. . . . The desire for a lifestyle of more goods and more leisure has increased "substantially". . . . Few think it is important to "help others," "correct social and economic inequalities" or "develop a meaningful philosophy of life." The young people . . . want their own children to have better opportunities than they did, but again think in terms of possessions.[13]

> If you look at our youth [in Spain], we're becoming a nation of narcissists, concerned mainly with the cult to the body, to comfort, to consumption, to money.[14]

It is the young who shape the future of human society. It does not bode well for its future if people become increasingly concerned with their materialistic self-interest, to the exclusion of collective concerns and societal needs. And effective planning is limited or impossible when the focus is on near-term satisfactions without regard to longer-range considerations. "No outward tinkering will improve this overpowered civilization, now plainly in the final and fossilized stage of its materialization. Nothing will produce an effective change but the fresh transformation that has already begun in the human mind."[15]

VULNERABILITY

Humans are vulnerable to the forces of earth and nature that cannot be controlled: drought, floods, earthquakes, volcanic eruptions, hurricanes, tornadoes, tsunamis. People around the world are continually subjected to one or more of these potentially catastrophic forces of nature. At the same time that the monsoon brings rain to irrigate the agricultural crops feeding hundreds of millions of people in the Far East, it floods large areas, destroys homes and crops, causing deaths, and displacing people. Famines occur in Africa, bringing death and destitution, with large migrations of people from the drought-stricken regions. Human responses to the destructive forces of nature are limited to reducing risks and damage by methods of construction, protective shelters, site selection, emergency relief, and insurance if available.

Man is vulnerable to a second set of dangers that he creates himself in the course of civilization. War and armed conflict are potentially the most destructive. By the turn of the century urbanization will place one-half of the world's population in a state of vulnerability that did not exist when people lived "on the farm" and were almost self-sufficient. City-dwellers are completely dependent on other people to supply them with imported food, water, clothing, shelter, energy, and other necessities of life. The successful functioning of urban transportation, communication, sanitation, and other service systems depends on operators other than the people who use them. Failure of a city's sources of supply or service systems can bring it to a grinding halt in a few days. With the population of some metropolitan urban areas approaching 30 million people, there is serious concern among public administrators that such large concentrations may be literally unmanageable: if so, with dire consequences for the health, safety, and welfare of their inhabitants. The global population explosion imposes severe stresses on the human species to provide food, shelter, gainful work, and health care for its multiplying numbers without lowering average living standards and depriving many people of essential sustenance.

The march of civilization is producing more actual and potential vulnerabilities for humans than it has eliminated in the past. Industrial activities are polluting the atmosphere: threatening the protective ozone layer, increasing the greenhouse effect warming the earth, producing damaging acid rain, contaminating land and water with radioactive, toxic, and infectious wastes and spills. Irreplaceable natural resources are being exhausted and many others are being used without regard for balancing depletion and replacement.

Scientific advances create new vulnerabilities. For example, existing varieties of wheat are replaced by a few new strains produced by genetic manipulation to have greater food value and greater resistance to damaging organisms. But widespread use of the new strains increases the possibility of the entire wheat crop being destroyed by a new disease or destructive pest. High-voltage lines transmitting electricity and electrical equipment of various kinds create electromagnetic fields that may injure humans and other animate life. Electronic computer systems, which are becoming an indispensable part of human activities, are vulnerable to surreptitious criminal and fraudulent use difficult to detect before damage has been done. In general, as the technical systems required for modern industrialized societies to function multiply and become more interdependent, they become more vulnerable to malicious disruption and terrorism—in sharp contrast with the simpler methods employed by less-complicated societies not long ago.

When human activities transgress fundamental characteristics and limitations of the natural world, we make ourselves susceptible to serious disruption or extinction as a species. Our increasing ability to shape the physical environment by engineering and affect the form of animate life by biological manipulation does not mean that we can constantly oppose or try to overpower nature and still survive as an animal species. We do not know how man-made changes will affect the almost infinite number of interrelated animate organisms and physical features that exist on earth with us. They may determine the future of life on earth as much as or more than human activities.

POPULATION GROWTH, MOVEMENT

Most of those observing the problems confronting the world today agree that explosive population growth constitutes or causes many of them. After many centuries of gradual growth, the world population has exploded from under 2 billion in 1929 to 5.5 billion in 1988. Of the approximately 6 billion people on earth today, 1 billion maintain a superior standard of living. The majority of 4 billion live with what they can afford with an average per capita wealth one-fiftieth that of the wealthier category. One billion people exist in "absolute poverty": too poor to buy enough food to retain their health or hold a job.

These disparities of income and condition are accentuated as population growth outstrips economic growth and there is no wider distribution of wealth. Society cannot or does not produce and distribute enough food, shelter, clothing, and health care to keep pace with population growth and assure the increasing percentage of the population who are young that they can anticipate an average standard of living no worse than that of their parents or grandparents. "To assure that the world is well on its way to sustainable development during the first part of the next century, a minimum of 3 percent annual per capita income growth will be necessary as well as greater equity in income distribution within developing countries."[16]

Those with a superior standard of living cling to it tenaciously or seek a still higher level. "People try to maintain their living standards even in hard times, and they don't ration their spending until they feel forced to do so."[17] Those who can afford only a minimum standard of living have neither the time nor the wherewithal to obtain an education. Without it, employment opportunities other than menial jobs are few and far between, and this segment of the population falls further behind as society becomes more complicated and technical.

The poorest countries are the fastest growing. Without their cooperation, global environmental problems will not be fully resolved. Normally, the governments of poor nations must seek to raise or at least retain the existing standard of living for their people individually and the nation as a whole to advance, to avoid widespread discontent, and to prevent a political or revolutionary change in government. To do this, they will insist that their industries produce at the lowest cost at the desired level of production without regard to any adverse effects. Cutting down the forests for firewood will continue regardless of resulting soil erosion, altered local weather patterns, and the destruction of a natural resource unless new trees are planted and nurtured until they are fully grown. Environmental movements will not prevail in developing countries unless those who determine policy are persuaded that immediate economic and political gains must not be allowed to pollute the air and water, destroy forests and topsoil, and otherwise misuse the basic resources of the nation.

In general, population growth stresses a society in various ways. More natural resources and manufactured products are needed to sustain more people. More of all kinds of pollution are produced. Besides condemning many people to starvation and poverty, population growth underlies virtually every environmental problem we face today. More people move to cities, magnifying the problems of urbanization and densification. Larger numbers of people are more difficult to manage and govern. Rapid growth means less time to absorb and adjust to change, to conduct current operations effectively, to plan ahead, and to effect improvements.

The movement of people involves planning in many ways. Transportation systems are provided as a principal element in city, state, regional, and national planning. Provisions are made for the movement of people in emergencies. Movement changes the mix of the population at the place of departure and at their destination. Immigration brings the customs and attitudes of ethnic minorities. The global movement of people contributes to the internationalization that is a primary economic force in the world today. It also has left few environments unaffected by the activities of man. Frequent movement is limited to relatively few people. Large-scale migrations are usually a result of war or other emergencies. Most people on earth never leave the area close by their birthplace or permanent home.

There are annual migrations of people between summer and winter habitats in the mountainous areas of developing countries, the flow of vacationers from northern to southern Europe, and a reverse flow of "foreign workers." The influx of vacationers from New York to Florida in the winter is a primary consideration for planning in Florida. Recent years have seen the migration of millions of people in Africa and Asia fleeing famine, driven from their homes by war and tribal conflict, or escaping political aggression and economic depression. From Afghanistan alone some 5 million refugees have fled during the past 12 years. Such events contribute to serious social unrest.

The decentralization of many of the manufacturing plants of the leading industrial nations to locations in other countries, and the internationalization of banking and finance, have greatly increased worldwide air travel by business and professional people. "In the zeal of even the most remote nations to attract tourist dollars, pounds, marks and francs, they have steadily depleted the number of untouched corners in the world."[18]

The United States probably has the most mobile population in the world. On the average, the American family moves its place of residence every five years or so, most often within the same city or state. This poses a particular problem for local planning in a democracy. Local legislators must be alert to changes in their constituents' opinions and preferences as part of the residential population in their electoral district moves away and is replaced by new voters every year. And the United States receives more immigrants from more different countries than any other nation. Aircraft, automobiles, and railroads throughout the world carry hundreds of millions of passengers on personal and business trips every hour of every day. In general, the movement of people reduces cultural isolation but not necessarily personal loneliness. The more people travel, the less local and limited their outlook and the broader their awareness—if not necessarily their understanding—of how other people live and think. Triggered perhaps by its adoption years ago for commercial air traffic control by all nations, English has become the most common language for world intercommunication. When formalized in 1992, the European Community will no longer require passport presentation or visas among its members.

The international movement of people and goods imposes a severe burden of accommodation upon countries receiving large numbers of illegal immigrants. Illegal drugs, animal and plant diseases, harmful insects, and other damaging organisms are transported in greater quantity and more rapidly than ever before. "The zebra mussel may be one of the greatest biological invaders in North America, ranking up there with the gypsy moth and the starling. . . . The most spectacular example of a whole slew of introductions happening all over the world, the result of ballast water."[19] Also, modern air transportation presents very vulnerable and tempting targets for terrorism. These developments constitute another set of problems requiring cooperative planning and action among nations, difficult to achieve under the most favorable circumstances.

BUREAUCRACY

Every large organization is a bureaucracy in that it consists of a body of employees who perform its regular operations. They are the long-term personnel who carry out the established activities of the government, business, or military organization. "Their purpose is to stabilize and routinize operations so that they can be carried out regularly and consistently. Also, to act as brakes allowing time for the desirability and feasibility of proposed changes to be tested or for their gradual absorption into the bureaucratic system to take place without severe disruption."[20] Major mistakes are minimized by successive review and actions conducted in accordance with formal procedures established gradually over the life of the organization. The knowledge concerning operations accumulated by bureaucrats over the years is passed on to their successors.

The term "bureaucracy" is associated today almost exclusively with government, disregarding the bureaucracies of business and those of the military services as distinct from civil government. Business and military organizations share most of the bureaucratic features of civil governmental bodies. But business bureaucracies functioning under capitalistic conditions are subject to competitive challenge in the commercial marketplace. Higher salaries and other forms of payment, bonuses, and stock options are probably greater incentives to self-improvement and better performance than government titles and military rank. Business also can relate advancement to sales or production quotas and other specific measures of performance not available in government. Perquisites and retirement benefits are available to both. Institutionally, government, business, and military bureaucracies have many more common characteristics than differences.

For a number of reasons, civil governmental bureaucracies are the most prone to crippling inefficiencies. To begin with, as part of the sovereign body they have to do with a broader spectrum of human affairs, considerations, and responsibilities than other organizations in a society. Their operations are correspondingly difficult and complex, all the more since political factors are more directly, forcefully, and continually involved in civil government than in business and the military services. The civil governmental bureaucracy serves many purposes besides its critical role in the conduct of human affairs. It is often bigger than needed for efficient operations because it is used as a base of political power or patronage by the ruling authority: to award supporters for past actions and assure their future loyalty, support, noninterference, or vote. Government bureaucracies constitute an important block of votes in democracies and a political force in other systems of government that seek incumbent authority and to perpetuate themselves. Without a limiting force, governmental bureaucracies continue to grow simply because many people prefer employment that is relatively permanent and undemanding. Bureaucracies are also a form of protection against political replacement and the rapid and disconcerting change that is more likely to occur in other elements of the society. There is little motivation for organizational and individual improvement because there are few incentives to advance. Promotion correlates closely with the length of satisfactory service. The status quo is the desirable state of affairs. Whistleblowers are discouraged, disregarded as malcontents, or penalized as disloyal and untrustworthy. These are common characteristics of governmental bureaucracies as a whole, not indictments of those individuals within them who perform with professional competence and conscientiousness.

In some countries bureaucracies are a way of providing "full employment" if this is the political policy or constitutional requirement. The Soviet Union and East Germany, before the dissolution of one and reunification of the other with West Germany, revealed the vast size and stagnant incompetence that can be attained by governmental bureaucracies. Their employees considered their jobs permanent and immune to challenge or change. Since the constitution of the People's Republic of China guarantees full employment, the government absorbs what the industrial and service sectors cannot. And in all three nations, the policy of overcentralized planning created oversize bureaucracies in a vain attempt to plan and direct industrial production and all other basic societal activities from their capitols: Moscow, East Berlin, and Beijing.

There is a momentum for all bureaucracies to grow, which must be taken into account by society. A few examples from the United States suffice to illustrate this trend. The combined staffs of the members of the U.S. House of Representatives and Senate have more than doubled during the past twenty years; "today's Congress is becoming a kind of bureaucracy itself."[21] The White House staff of the president has grown from a core of 14 persons in 1945 to 568 people in 1989. The Pentagon—the world's largest office building—houses some 25,000 of the military and civilian staff employees of the U.S. Department of Defense who oversee the operations of over 2 million military personnel at the present time. An exceptional example of bureaucratic duplication occurred at a U.S. Army post during the Vietnam War when 22,000 Vietnamese were employed as support staff for 26,000 Americans who were themselves supposed to be support troops. Despite the avowed intentions of recent presidents and legislators to reduce the size of government, federal, state, and local bureaucracies continue to grow: to accommodate an increasing population, to serve special bureaucratic purposes as noted above, and in part because of the tendency to add more people in a period of expansion than are really needed.

Businesses expand for the same reasons except that purely political padding is less a factor, if it exists at all. Eventually, general economic conditions or direct competition force businesses to pare the "fat" that often results from the built-in momentum of growth. "The new chairman of the General Motors Corporation . . . said GM would try and remove layers of bureaucracy and give more decision-making power to lower-level workers."[22] Nonprofit organizations also exhibit excessive bureaucratic expansion. For example, in the decade 1975–85 college administrative staffs increased by almost two-thirds, many times more than the modest increases in the faculty and student body during the same period. "Congressional logrolling, bitter service rivalries and massive bureaucratic inertia are the enemies of military preparedness, blocking reforms that are desperately needed to prepare the military for the 1990s and beyond."[23]

Increased bureaucratic complexity is apparent to every American taxpayer in the forms and procedures that are required. A recent commissioner of the U.S. Internal Revenue Service agrees that "the tax law, in large part, may no longer be administrable by the IRS and no longer comprehensible by most taxpayers and many of their advisors."[24] Business and individuals are reported to have spent in 1984 more than 1.8 billion hours filling out government forms. For their part, bureaucracies are producing increasingly legalistic and complicated documents and communications of many kinds that are incomprehensible to most people.

A "document request" by the chairman of the U.S. Senate Judiciary Committee addressed to a nominee for the U.S. Court of Appeals in Washington, D.C., is a supreme example of "information overkill." It contains twelve sections with an average of ten or more subsections asking for an incredible list of documents, memoranda, correspondence, law cases and actions explaining and justifying a wide range of personal and organizational activities extending back more than five years. A final section lists eight Instructions and Definitions. The document request, published in its entirety in the *Wall Street Journal*, must be seen to be believed.[25] It illustrates the extent to which bureaucratic complexity can be carried out by an overzealous and unrealistic staff: providing reason enough for the nominee either to refuse to reply to such a burdensome inquiry, or to withdraw his name from consideration if he is sufficiently disillusioned with government by such excess.

GLOBAL CLIMATE

Only recently has the possibility of significant change in the world's climate come to the attention of the public. Although it will be some years before a sufficient record of change is accumulated to confirm current conclusions beyond question, most of the scientific community believe that human activities are causing climatic changes that can have profound effects on life on earth.

Emission of chlorofluorocarbons from industrial plants and the widespread use of manufactured products using aerosols are affecting the layer of ozone in the upper atmosphere of the earth. As this protective layer is dissipated, more ultraviolet light from the sun reaches the earth, causing cancers in humans and severely damaging aquatic life, agricultural crops, and forests. It appears that this is occurring now over the south pole— an area geographically remote from human habitation, but an important breeding place for the microscopic photoplankton on which numerous aquatic animals feed. The combustion of fossil fuels in automobiles, aircraft, and industrial processes around the world increases the amount of methane and carbon dioxide in the upper atmosphere. This causes the infrared heat rays showering the earth from the sun to reflect back to earth from the layer of chemical intensification, rather than redirected back into outer space. This situation appears to be warming the earth and its thin atmospheric covering on which all animate and vegetative life depends.

Both of these environmental developments present serious problems for human survival. Depletion of the ozone layer injures people by causing more cancers, damages agricultural crops, and blights the earth's forests, which affect global and regional weather and supply a wide range of natural products. Further warming of the earth and its atmosphere will damage or destroy animate organisms that can exist only within a range of temperatures, and there is not enough time for evolutionary adjustment to temperatures beyond these limits. If the earth is warmed enough to melt its polar ice caps, the water level of the oceans will rise many feet, flooding coastline areas along all the continents and countries fronting on the seas. Since many of the major cities of the world are located in whole or in part along the coast, a mammoth urban relocation would be necessary over a period of years before the forthcoming flooding. The dwelling places of many millions of people and hundreds of thousands of productive facilities would have to be rebuilt above the new oceanic waterline.

These environmental developments illustrate the sensitive interrelationships that exist between man and nature. The effects of human activities on the natural environment intensify as the world population increases and science and technology continue to produce new processes and products. Familiar examples include the expanding use of fossil fuels and radioactive materials, production of toxic and other waste, accelerated soil erosion, cutting down forests, nuclear power generation, and the capability of employing nuclear explosions for peaceful as well as military purposes. The precise impact of genetic engineering and other biological manipulation on the environment remains to be seen, but it will be extensive. While the separate effects of many human activities have been made clear in recent years, their combined impact is not clear. It may be greater than the simple sum of its parts.

What is becoming apparent is the subtle and complex web of interrelationships and the precarious balance that exists between man and nature. Changes in this situation by thoughtless or faulty human activities can significantly affect the present condition and future prospects of people as a species. Recent studies of the physical development of the earth and the evolution of animate life in the past reveal that small changes have triggered or halted evolutionary advances. In the eyes of its human occupants the world is spatially enormous, with vast expanses of oceans and land constituting a seemingly unalterable inertia. This view discounts the dependence of animate and vegetative life on a most delicate balance of natural forces that apply globally or to very large areas.

ENVIRONMENTAL POLLUTION

The earliest animate life had to adjust to hostile atmospheric conditions during the physical formation of the earth over hundreds of millions of years. Volcanic gases are hostile to animal and vegetative life nearby.

"The Hawaiian Thoracic Society has urged residents to take precautions during heavy vog episodes [volcanic gaseous emissions] like wearing surgical masks and staying indoors with air conditioning."[26] Most recently, radon gas formed by natural substances within the earth has been identified as harmful to human health above a certain concentration. The extensive and increasing environmental pollution brought about by humans is very recent historically, but actually and potentially more devastating than the few forms of "natural" pollution. It has been called to public attention in recent years by reports in the mass media of oil spills, smog, nuclear contamination, sewage and waste disposal, acid rain, water pollution, and years ago by the discovery that the insecticide DDT was being absorbed in the tissues of aquatic animal life in the oceans around the world.

The costs of prevention and clean-up escalate as human activities continue to pollute the land, water, and atmosphere on which our survival and well-being depend. Many billions of dollars must be spent to control known sources of pollution, and additional billions to neutralize dangerous waste sites created in the past—unless the deaths, injury, and damage they cause are accepted as a necessary aspect of life. There are many kinds of pollution to be considered. Nuclear accidents endanger people nearby and contaminate large areas with radioactive fallout blown by the winds. Untreated chemical emissions from the smokestacks of copper smelters and other industrial plants damage plant life downwind, and accumulate in the atmosphere to form acid rain, injuring vegetation and destroying vulnerable animal life. Emissions from smokestacks in the European low countries have destroyed fish life in 1,800 lakes in Norway. Toxic wastes and raw sewage can pollute surface waters. Underground aquifers, which provide half of the nation's drinking water, have been contaminated in most of the United States by human, industrial, and agricultural wastes. Some eighty countries, supporting 40 percent of the world's population, suffer from serious water shortage. Smog is a health hazard for the inhabitants of many large cities in different parts of the world. It also damages certain architectural surface materials and ornaments exposed to its erosive action. More than one-half of the U.S. population lives in communities polluted by injurious smog.

Electromagnetic radiation from some industrial facilities utilizing or transporting high voltages and manufactured products such as microwave ovens and television sets may be hazardous to the health of people who are close by for considerable periods of time. Frequent oil spills and the emptying of the ballast tanks of ships pollutes the ocean where this occurs, and are probably slowly raising the general level of pollution throughout the vast expanse of the oceans. This average pollution will be further increased when the hundreds of thousands of metal drums containing radioactive waste with a long half-life, dumped in the ocean without concern for the future, rust through and spill their contents into the water. The industrial effluents that deplete the ozone layer and increase the greenhouse reflection in the earth's upper atmosphere—discussed in the previous section on climatic change—are second in their impact only to the potentially destructive and contaminative consequences of a global war employing nuclear weapons.

Disposal of ordinary or "normal" industrial and household waste becomes a pollution problem when populations and heavy industrial activities increase and disposable income allows an accumulation of material goods. In the wealthier and highly industrialized countries—especially in the United States—the disposal of refuse is a national problem. Refuse includes waste from industrial processes, debris from construction projects, discarded automobiles, infectious medical materials, and household trash and garbage. "American drivers threw out 279 million tires [in 1989]. These tires joined 2.5 billion to 3 billion others already choking land fills and blighted roadsides, vacant lots, and riverbanks where they attract disease carrying mosquitos and pose fire hazards."[27] The amount of household waste relates not only to affluence but also to urbanization. In towns and cities, disposal of waste by individuals is not feasible, as it is for farm families and others living in the countryside. Recycling of refuse and use of biodegradable materials is a recent effort in some countries. Conservation and the substitution of products that do not produce disposal problems has hardly begun. In the United States, nearby landfill sites for urban refuse are full, and it must be transported further and further away at greater expense to areas that do not welcome urban dumps in their "back yard." Newspaper readers and television viewers in the United States recall the barge that travelled up and down the inland waterways off the East Coast for a month or more several years ago seeking someone on shore to accept the refuse. It could not be legally dumped at sea.

The impact of problems associated with pollution extend beyond the immediate costs of devising means of control and enforcing programs of prevention. To store dangerous radioactive and toxic wastes and clean up existing waste sites presenting a hazard to human health will require many billions of dollars that will not be available for other uses. To eliminate smog in some cities will require changes in human habits and existing pricing policies as well as mechanical and material controls. It may not be possible to maintain disposable income and the present standard of living during the period of extra-heavy expenditures required to clean up past mistakes and control pollution previously ignored. The human species may have to go through a period of arrested development or retrenchment while it eliminates or reduces those of its activities that are deteriorating the environment and, to the extent possible, restores places already damaged or destroyed.

Underlying the present situation is the reluctance of government and particularly elected officials to acknowledge the extent and dangers of progressive pollution and act to remove or reduce past misdeeds.

> In the course of producing plutonium for World War II and the cold war that followed, the Hanford Works released radioactive wastes totaling millions of curies. The facility released billions of gallons of liquids and billions of cubic meters of gases containing contaminants, including plutonium and other radionuclides. . . . Scientists and policy makers never informed the residents of the region of the emissions or warned them of any potential or real dangers, even when the releases far exceeded the "tolerance levels" or "allowable limits" defined as safe at the time. Instead, on many occasions they told the public that Hanford's operations were controlled and harmless.[28]

Most pollutants are slow acting, taking longer periods of time to damage or destroy than the incumbencies of lifetimes of politicians who avoid unpleasant or difficult subjects to the extent possible and postpone decisions that might threaten their reelection. Bureaucracies favor the status quo, avoiding or delaying actions to resolve challenging and disturbing problems. People in general prefer not to recognize unpleasant facts or to underestimate their implications, especially those involving the longer-range future and affecting others rather than themselves directly and immediately. "Sufficient unto the day is the evil thereof."[29] Also, most people in the world do not comprehend the significance of pollution problems; they are preoccupied with the difficulties of daily living. And developing nations promoting increased industrial activity to raise the average standard of living, to compete commercially with other countries, or to acquire greater political or military power consider the perils of pollution secondary to rapid uncontrolled industrialization.

FAILURE OF GOVERNMENT

The overall state of a society depends on any one of many factors, but the most important is almost always the nature and effectiveness of its government: the official leadership and its supporting bureaucracy, which are the sovereign controlling forces. Sometimes a society is directly or indirectly controlled by an individual or group outside the official government. When this is the case, the term governance designates this form of unofficial government. For example, the activities of primitive societies often were directed as much by the shaman—the medicine man and interpreter of magical forces—as by a council of elders comprising the supreme tribal authority. A corporation, other organization, or individual whose activities and decisions determine community life is in fact the governing body rather than the official local government. In times past and in Iran today religious figures may dominate the government of a nation.

Except in the smallest societies, there are, of course, several levels of government: the sovereign or highest (national or federal), intermediate (state or region), and local (town, city, county, district). In the United States five levels of government are involved: federal, state, county, district, and municipal or township. In at least one state, a sixth level of regional government has been added. Each of these levels has its area of jurisdiction and authority determined by the national government. Local governments confront the day-to-day problems and needs of people most directly. They are subject to immediate and pressing public reaction when the essentials of daily life such as food, water, shelter, or civil order are affected. Or when an established high standard of living is threatened. Each successive higher level of government is concerned with broader socioeconomic considerations affecting larger areas; its laws and policies direct the next lower level of government. Certain functions of government are performed most successfully at the national level: for example, the monetary system, military defenses, tax collection, nationwide communication.

The tasks of government are correspondingly more complicated and difficult than in simpler societies in the past. This trend will continue with societies becoming more complex and harder to manage, possibly with a corresponding decrease in productive performance, unless governmental administration improves enough to compensate. As the size of bureaucracies increases to match population increases, regardless of need, governmental administration is made more difficult for this reason alone. In general, larger organizations are harder to manage than smaller ones. If the growth of governmental bureaucracies is for political purposes rather than a response to increased demand for services, effective performance is even less likely. If the ability of individual bureaucrats is no greater, the collective competence of the larger group is reduced. And if governmental "management by crisis" continues to be the prevailing option in the United States, the possibilities of effective action are reduced accordingly by the simple but crucial fact that conditions have been allowed to deteriorate to such a point that eventual improvement is more difficult and costly. The advantages of planning and anticipatory action before a crisis develops are lost. An ounce of prevention has not been provided to avoid the pound of cure. In many instances, belated mitigation rather than cure is all that is possible after a potentially catastrophic situation has been allowed to develop.

The success or failure of autocratic governments is evaluated by the ruling authority. The populace has little or nothing to say or to do, other than to commend for the purposes of ingratiation or to complain within the limits permitted. In freer societies the reputation of the government is affected by its external image in the eyes of the public, and its internal image in the minds of its members. If it is regarded as a "necessary evil," to be minimized to the extent possible in favor of corporate and individual enterprise, it cannot fulfill its societal responsibilities. If it is respected as a body of trained professionals performing essential and desirable activities in the public interest, it is a source of pride as a major force determining the current well-being and future prospects of the society. Of course, image and reality have a reciprocal relationship. A poor image may be the result of poor performance; it also makes it harder to attract the quality of people needed to improve the discredited bureaucracy. A favorable reputation is the consequence of effective performance; it attracts capable people and in so doing further strengthens the operations and image of an already successful bureaucracy. As discussed later in Chapter 4, treatment of the government by the mass media of communication can affect or determine its image. In some governments its employees are motivated by concern with the general public welfare or by professional interest in a particular function or activity of government. In others, governmental employment is a sinecure. Examples of the many different kinds of government and the wide range of special situations are to be found around the world. Bureaucracies range from the professional, efficient, and effective to incompetent, bloated, and corrupt.

Governmental management by crisis relates to the close and continuous contact that has been established between elected representatives and their constituents by the mass media of communication, by reduced travel times, and by the high cost of election and reelection. And as discussed in Chapter 2 on human characteristics, politicians are aware that the body politic does not want to be confronted with problems, unpleasant realities, change, or any sacrifice. Accordingly, politicians are all too often unwilling to anticipate, plan ahead, or even acknowledge serious societal problems until they become so intolerable that they can no longer be ignored. The political consequences of current crises are less than the political advantage of disregarding critical problems to the extent possible and postponing necessary action until the last possible minute. Needless to say, such belated concern and forced action must cope with problems when they have become almost intractable, requiring more resources, more drastic action, and causing greater social instability than would have been the case had they been addressed earlier.

The cost of election and reelection to political office is forcing our elected representatives to spend as much or more time obtaining campaign funds than they devote to the process of governing, their primary responsibility. U.S. senators and representatives are now in their Washington offices an average of four days a week with weekends and recesses totaling several months to return home, maintain local contacts, and campaign for the next election. Public appearances and other activities relating to reelection take up additional time when they are in Washington. The importance of this continuous campaigning is confirmed by the 95 percent rate of reelection of incumbents. The cost in time and money of unseating them is prohibitive for all but the very wealthy, or someone supported by special interests willing to provide whatever money it takes for their candidate to be elected. This situation increases the average age of elected officials and decreases the rate of turnover and infusion of new people and ideas.

A consequence of these developments is that little time is left to analyze major problems confronting the government, determine what can and should be done, evaluate plans for improvement, devise legislation and programs of action to achieve necessary and desirable objectives, and monitor results. This primary purpose of government is receiving less and less attention and effort as problems multiply and become more severe. "Too many legislators pay more attention to the next election than to current legislative matters. It is impossible to be a good candidate and a good legislator simultaneously."[30] Election now depends on money provided by special interests and politically supportive groups to pay for the necessary television time, other mass media exposure, public opinion polls, and the professional political consultants who are now an essential part of the elective process in the United States.

Accepting this money necessarily incurs some indebtedness on the part of the recipient. Many legislators maintain that this is no more than an obligation to meet with and listen to the views and special desires of major campaign contributors. That more than access and a receptive ear are usually involved is revealed almost daily in newspapers and on television. Within the past several years the Speaker of the U.S. House of Representatives resigned and a senior senator was censured because of unethical actions in connection with political donations. A U.S. senator was "strongly and severely reprimanded" for his linkage of fund raising and official activities in behalf of a savings and loan association. Probably most politicians whose election depends on such funds provided by special interests and political action groups have at one time or another favored legislation or taken other action in behalf of large contributors. And each member of a legislative body defers to certain political preferences of the others in a quid pro quo interrelationship.

Corruption has existed throughout history. As discussed in the next chapter, it is latent in human behavior. Official misconduct is therefore an existing or potential problem in all governments. It appears to be on the rise in the United States.

A federal grand jury indicted five state legislators . . . accusing them of accepting bribes in exchange for their support legalizing betting on horses and greyhounds.[31]

Federal prosecutors have identified six more present or former members of
the . . . legislature as "known conspirators" in a bribery investigation.[32]

There have been 18 months of scandals in high places, a fireworks of sex,
stupidity and greed extraordinary even for this notoriously corrupt state . . .
hauling off the treasurer, the attorney general, two state representatives,
the Senate majority leader and two Senate presidents. . . . The governor from
1969 to 1977 and then again from 1985 to 1989, pleaded guilty to five counts
of extortion, fraud, and obstruction of justice.[33]

The huge amounts of money involved in drug trafficking are causing
widespread corruption, allegedly extending to the last bastion of governmental probity: the federal judiciary. Malfeasance in government is probably greater at the federal and state levels than in localities. As noted
previously local politicians are under closer scrutiny. But there are many
examples of land-use zone changes and other actions by local legislators
relating to real estate development that are demonstrably linked with
campaign contributions. "In 10 instances . . . developers sharply increased
contributions about the time a key project [requiring approval] reached
the Board of Estimate."[34] Legislation, approvals, and bureaucratic actions
of various kinds occur unobtrusively favoring political donors and organizations capable of delivering a significant block of votes. Witness the
allegations of corruption under investigation in the award of contracts by
the U.S. Department of Housing and Urban Development and procure-
ment by the Department of Defense during the 1980s.
Malfeasance is by no means limited to governments. It is shared by
business and other elements of society. "Serious criminal fraud [was]
discovered at 60 percent of the savings institutions seized by the government in 1989—triple the fraud rate in failures of commercial banks."[35]
Most issues of the *Wall Street Journal* contain reports of fraud and criminal acts within the business world. Corruption has extended to religious
leaders and institutions. Many of the ethical derelictions in private enterprise and other nongovernmental institutions are part of or contribute
to corruption in government. "The generic drug industry is corrupted by
companies that took shortcuts to get drugs approved, including bribing
regulators and submitting false data on equivalency and effectiveness."[36]
The political system in the United States has changed markedly during
the past several generations. When the population was much smaller and
large urban concentrations far fewer, more direct citizen participation in
the political process was possible than is the case today. In smaller communities, town meetings provided direct contact between constituents
and their elected representatives in the actual conduct of government—
as they still do in towns in several states. The issues were simpler and
comprehensible to the electorate. Newspapers, magazines, and word of

mouth were the main means of disseminating information and formulating individual and public opinion. Nowadays there are more than 250 million people in the United States. Two-thirds of them live in cities and metropolitan regions. The nation and the world have changed as a result of scientific and technical advances and a great expansion of international economic ties. Television and radio operate in the average household every day for hours on end.

Voters communicate their attitudes, opinions, and specific desires to elected representatives by direct contact, by their actions, and their responses to various forms of inquiry. The public at large expresses its views and desires continually through news reports, articles, and broadcasts of many kinds and the results of public opinion polls disseminated by the mass media. At prescribed times the voting public expresses its opinion of the performance of elected representatives at the ballot box.

> From representatives who could vote and act beyond current opinion when they believed this was in the best interest of their constituency or the public at large, they have become middlemen and women who translate multiple public opinions and special interests into legislation and other political action.[37]

Fifty years ago a leading authority on public opinion could demonstrate that the collective judgment of the American people was superior to that expressed by their political leaders: not only because of people's common sense and insight, but also because of their greater willingness to acknowledge and face reality than their elected representatives who were politically reluctant to take a stand until problems become intolerable. Today, common sense and ordinary insight are not enough.

> Politicians often make critical decisions about issues ranging from the proliferation of nuclear missiles to AIDS in nearly total ignorance of the technical aspects of the problems involved. At the same time the scientists and technologists that politicians need to rely on for technical advice frequently have little grasp of the manifold social and political consequences of their discoveries.[38]

The electorate must consider, formulate an opinion, and vote on a range of issues much more complicated than those confronting it fifty years ago. Also, with the increasing cultural diversity of the American electorate, specific propositions to be voted on and related political statements may be misunderstood. And with the average level of education and comprehension of native Americans decreasing, political material may be misinterpreted or even incomprehensible for a significant segment of the body politic. Political discussion that helps people understand the issues on which they are asked to vote is almost nonexistent today, except among those connected with a candidate's election or reelection, special interests, and groups organized for preconceived political presentation and discussion. Elected officials are selected by a smaller and smaller percentage of eligible voters.

In the United States the voter is faced with a difficult choice. On the one hand, the mass media of communication have expanded the awareness and concern of individual citizens with regard to a range of local, national, and even international problems once regarded as the province and responsibility of government and interested professional groups: for example, drugs, diseases, environmental pollution, tax policy, the homeless, and various issues raised in referendums and recalls submitted to voters in the states permitting these forms of direct vote. On the other hand, the electorate is being called on to vote on matters so unfamiliar, specialized, or technical that even well-informed and highly educated persons do not feel competent to vote intelligently. "Voters across the country have put at least 67 proposals on the statewide ballots for Tuesday's elections [November 6, 1990], the largest number in more than five decades."[39] There is no practical way for these people to obtain the background information needed in such situations without spending more time for personal investigation than most people can afford.

The voter is the object of constant efforts to influence him or her: by political statements and allegations on television and radio and in newspapers, periodicals, and mass mailings, paid for by the opposing candidates for elective office, political parties, and special interests. These statements often contradict each other as to facts, each claiming to be the accurate and truthful account. Collectively, the voter is the object of the best "market analysis" available concerning how he can be induced to respond politically in the desired way. Unknown to most people, an increasing proportion of news reports, stories, and studies carried by the mass media of communication are the product in whole or in part of statements by organizations with a vested interest expressing their particular view, or news service reports used by most newspapers and broadcast stations. Both of the predetermined inputs are often reproduced verbatim or used as the basis for "rewrites."

Many voters are disillusioned by the performance of their elected representatives, as discussed above, and by the intense rivalry of the political parties, which causes them to concentrate on adversarial tactics, unable to respond constructively to issues of primary public concern. Political deadlock often prevents our elected representatives from performing their primary responsibility of resolving crucial issues, requiring the electorate to assume this responsibility themselves when possible by initiative and referendum. And redrawing the boundaries of electoral districts after each decennial census requires recourse to the courts because the political parties cannot reach agreement. To make matters worse, most voters do not care enough to insist that politicians act thoughtfully and wisely in the public interest on important governmental matters, but judge them according to "what have you done for me lately?" The percentage of people in the United States who vote is decreasing. More and more young people do not regard voting as an obligation in a democratic society, or believe it is largely a useless exercise because political decisions are made by the powers that be with little regard for the electorate except how they vote. "As citizens in a democracy, we have been the authors of the situation we are in, and we won't begin to find our way out until we begin to demand a style of governance that emphasizes both accountability and steadfast commitment to long-term goals."[40]

Voters' attitudes and conclusions are shaped, if not determined, by the information they receive through the mass media, discussed in Chapter 4. Present political processes do not provide enough information and analysis to understand the key problems confronting us and vote intelligently on particular proposals. There is no general indication of the interrelationships between different issues, problems, or events, of how a vote on one affects others, whether a proposed program of action contradicts prior commitments, or whether it is within the current capability of the society to perform. "The United States is becoming increasingly difficult to govern. . . . There is a consensus that no coalition of interests is strong enough to set priorities for the overall public good, to effect reforms that have a wide public support, to root out inefficiency and corruption in political leadership."[41]

A serious failure of government in the United States is inadequate presidential leadership in domestic public affairs. Of course presidents must pay close attention to and act with respect to crisis conditions within the country that threaten societal stability and the president's political future. And as commander in chief, a president must concentrate on the conduct of wars in which the United States is engaged. Apart from such situations, American presidents have been preoccupied in recent years with foreign affairs. They do not involve to anywhere near the same extent the different opinions, emotional reactions, political controversies, and multitude of diverse interests, actors, and adversarial conflicts characteristic of domestic affairs in democratic societies. Nor do foreign affairs normally raise the kind of domestic issues that can threaten a president's reelection. It is a relief to put aside, at least for a while, the difficulties of reliable analysis and constructive action associated with the critical domestic problems that are always present and never resolved to everyone's satisfaction. Foreign travel in specially designed U.S. Air Force One is divertive, interesting, and stimulating: meeting with other heads of state, royally received with respect if not deference. Small wonder that presidents enjoy conducting foreign affairs themselves within the White House, with less and less reliance on the Department of State. If this avoids the personal commitments and executive activities required to resolve troublesome domestic problems, so much better for their political survival.

Preoccupation with foreign affairs precludes the president from assuming societal, political, and operational leadership in domestic affairs as the sole elected representative of all the people in the nation: focusing public attention on critical problems, formulating policies, overseeing the preparation of plans, taking and promoting action by every means at his disposal. This is particularly true in the United States. With fifty states with the same constitutional rights but socioeconomically different, leadership is crucial to achieving the coordination of effort necessary for effective planning and actions to resolve national problems and national needs. This may be politically dangerous for the president, but it is operationally necessary. Planning for any society or organization is ineffective unless it is conducted by or closely associated with its chief executive.

Members of Congress also like to get away from the problems they continually face at home, by making inspection trips abroad singly or in groups as members of a congressional committee. State, county, and municipal legislators, governors, and other local officials take fact-finding or promotional trips to "sister" cities and comparable governmental agencies, paid for from public funds. To what extent this divertive interest in affairs away from home exists as a political syndrome outside the United States is known to those familiar with governmental practices in other parts of the world.

The major problems discussed in this chapter are imposing and discouraging when viewed together. Additional difficulties confronting man could be added. They have existed throughout human history, some of them in much milder form or with far less societal impact than is the case today when population growth and industrial-technological development have vastly increased the consequences of these problems and their effect on the future of Homo sapiens. If ignored they will surely create crisis conditions. If they are not resolved, they could be a major factor in the demise of the human species on this planet. They constitute the principal challenge to our society. They are primary objectives for our effort to steadily improve our current condition, our prospects, and our survival.

REFERENCES

1. Shakespeare, William, *Hamlet*, Act V. Sc. 1.
2. Schneider, Keith, "Scientist Who Managed to 'Shock the World' on Atomic Workers' Health," *New York Times*, 3 May 1990, p. 14 Z.
3. Nolan, James E., and Albert D. Wheelon, "Third World Ballistic Missiles," *Scientific American*, August 1990, pp. 34–37.

4. Goodman, Walter, "Horror of Mozambique's Civil War," *New York Times*, 2 March 1990, p. B 22K.
5. Johnson, Dirk, "In U.S. Parks, Some Seek a Retreat but Find Crime," *New York Times*, 21 August 1990, p. 1.
6. Hinds, Michael deCourey, "Number of Killings Soars in Big Cities across U.S.," *New York Times*, 18 July 1990, p. Z A1.
7. Smith, Wilbur E., "Liberté, Egalité, Fraternité," *National Geographic*, July 1989, p. 5.
8. Dowdney, A. K., "Mathematical Recreation," *Scientific American*, March 1990, p. 118.
9. Ehrlich, Paul R., and Anne H. Ehrlich, *The Population Explosion* (New York: Simon and Schuster, 1990), p. 140.
10. "Traditional Households Are Fading World-Wide," *Wall Street Journal*, 4 May 1990, p. B1.
11. "Never-Married Women Rearing More Children," *New York Times*, 2 August 1990, p. Z C3.
12. *Webster's New International Dictionary* (Springfield: Merriam, Second Edition, 1960) S.V. "materialism," p. 1514.
13. Otten, Alan, "The '80s Materialism Marks American Youth," *Wall Street Journal*, 16 May 1990, p. B1.
14. de Miguel, Amando, quoted in Riding, Alan, "Politics? The Generation Gap Yawns," *New York Times*, 17 June 1991, p. A4 Z.
15. Mumford, Lewis, quoted in Brendan Gill, "The Skyline: Homage to Mumford," *New Yorker*, 2 March 1990, p. 93.
16. MacNeill, Jim, "Strategies for Sustainable Economic Development," *Scientific American*, September 1989, p. 156.
17. Uchitelle, Louis, "So Far, No Shock for Consumers," *New York Times*, 30 July 1990, p. C2 Z.
18. "Tourist Boom: New Wealth and Woes," *Los Angeles Times*, 31 July 1990, p. H1.
19. Roberts, Leslie, "Zebra Mussel Invasion Threatens U.S. Waters," *Science*, 21 September 1990, p. 1370.
20. Branch, Melville C., *Planning: Universal Process* (New York: Praeger, 1990), p. 149.
21. Farney, Dennis, "A Bureaucracy Grows in Congress as Panels and Staffs Mushroom," *Wall Street Journal*, 18 December 1979, p. 1.
22. Levin, Don, "New Chairman of G.M. Promises Period of Stability," *New York Times*, 8 February 1990, p. Z C3.
23. Pasztor, Andy, and John J. Fialka, "U.S. Military Lacks Some Tools It Needs in the Mideast Crisis," *Wall Street Journal*, 28 August 1990, p. 1.
24. Stout, Hilary, "Tax Law Is Growing Ever More Complex, Outcry Ever Louder," *Wall Street Journal*, 12 April 1990, p. A1.
25. "Senator Biden Checks a Judicial Nominee," *Wall Street Journal*, 17 January 1990, p. A16.
26. Reinhold, Robert, "Volcanic Gases Fouling Once-Clear Air of Hawaii," *New York Times*, 7 May 1990, p. Z A13.
27. Feder, Barnaby J., "Shrinking the Old-Tire Mountain: Progress Slow," *New York Times*, 9 May 1990, p. Z C1.

28. Stenehjem, Michele, "Indecent Exposure," *Natural History*, September 1990, p. 6.
29. Matt. 6:34.
30. Unruh, Jesse, reported in "State Legislature Weakened, Political Science Students Told," *Trojan Family*, 10 July 1979, p. 20.
31. "What's News—, World-Wide," *Wall Street Journal*, 27 August 1990, p. 1.
32. "Six More Carolina Lawmakers Are Named in Bribe Inquiry," *New York Times* 12 September 1990, p. Z A17.
33. Bearak, Barry, "Corruption Runs Thick as Coal Dust," *Los Angeles Times*, 8 July 1990, p. 1.
34. Barbanel, Josh, "Abundant Political Gifts by Developers Faulted," *New York Times*, 27 November 1985, p. Y16.
35. Hayes, Thomas C., "Former Saving Executive Sentenced to 30 Years in Jail," *New York Times*, 6 April 1990, p. C1 Z.
36. Leary, Warren E., "More Charges Expected in Generic Drug Inquiry," *New York Times*, 20 December 1990, p. C2 Z.
37. Branch, Melville C., *Planning: Universal Process*, p. 184.
38. Ornstein, Robert, and Paul Ehrlich, *New World, New Mind* (New York: Doubleday, 1990), p. 64.
39. Pear, Robert, "Number of Ballot Initiatives Is the Greatest since 1932," *New York Times*, 5 November 1990, p. Z A15.
40. "Notes and Comment," *New Yorker*, 27 August 1990, p. 28.
41. Herbers, John, "Deep Government Disunity Alarms Many U.S. Leaders," *New York Times*, 12 November 1978, pp. 1, 74.

2

HUMAN CHARACTERISTICS AFFECTING PLANNING

The great virtue of pessimism is that it looks at reality and forces individuals, or a nation, to recognize their serious problems. A sound balance between optimism and pessimism can lead to both realism and constructive action, rather than an evasion of problems by happy-talk and wish-think.

Leonard Silk
New York Times (February 1991)

When we look at ourselves in the mirror we see a human being, a member of the species Homo sapiens: with self-awareness, the capacity to think, to consciously remember, to communicate by language, and to act toward designated objectives. Together with these mental capabilities we have the physical attributes of a species of animal that has evolved over a period of several million years, with roots extending much further back in evolutionary time. We are subject to our evolutionary development in the form and functioning of our bodies. Prosthesis and genetic manipulation enable us to alter our bodies in some respects beyond evolutionary limits, but as animals we are still subject to evolutionary restraints and requirements. One part of us is primitive and instinctual, the other the product of a brief 10,000 years of civilization with its leap forward in knowledge and the capability to produce a multitude of products, large projects, and complex systems of our devising. No other animal species is blessed or burdened with such a dual set of individual and societal characteristics. Therein lies our major problem or our primary prospect.

As an animal species we are a societal entity of over 5 billion individuals who are interrelated and interdependent in various ways. Although we differ from one another more than any other species, there are certain basic similarities in the form, functioning, and behavior of all of us that are probably necessary for us to endure as a species. The well-being and prospects of societies depend on a constructive behavioral relationship between individuals and the collective entity.

INDIVIDUAL CHARACTERISTICS

The individual characteristics of people discussed in *Planning: Universal Process* are among those associated with our evolutionary development—initially by chemical and biological reaction to the environment, and later as intuitive adjustments to environmental changes to ensure replication during many million years. Self-interest, fear of risk, territoriality, and anxiety when facing the unfamiliar are intrinsic forces that have favored the survival of animal species and societies. While the word prejudice implies a conscious reaction or attitude in humans, in other animals it is an instinctive avoidance of incompatible or potentially competitive societies or species. Human reactions today may be more instinctive than we realize. Research indicates that we may form likes or dislikes before our conscious minds are aware of our instinctive reaction and prejudicial conclusion.

Other inherent characteristics of individuals noted in the above book also relate to planning and survival. Faced with extinction if they did not react, the earliest humans adjusted quickly to existing conditions. They could only hope that by worshipful or ceremonial acts they might propitiate the natural or godly forces that determined their fate. In countries with primitive or precarious economies, only a few of the most serious societal problems can be considered. In developed countries many crucial issues can be ignored at least for a while without immediate threat to the society. People can avoid the emotional discomfort of having to address major problems by refusing to acknowledge that they exist. Or they can ignore the situation with the wishful hope that somehow their children or grandchildren will resolve the problems passed on to them by the current generation, even though the problems will have become much worse and the cost of correction much greater. The human tendency to accept "false precision"—to falsify by pretensions of accuracy that are not supported by statistical calculation or analytical reasoning—also is rooted in our emotional desire to maintain certain of our beliefs and wishes regardless of factual or rational justification. Our attitudes and actions also vary with our "perception of time": whether in general we look primarily to the past, the present, or the future.

Emotional forces within us frequently conflict with the rational thought and scientific method that are features of civilized society. Often we want to react to situations in ways that are emotionally satisfying but neither rationally appropriate nor operationally productive. Or we react in ways we claim are sensible when in fact they represent emotional needs within us which we do not recognize consciously, or they involve matters that we repress from our conscious awareness because emotionally we want to ignore or forget them.

To the extent individual characteristics that are not collectively constructive dominate human attitudes and actions, society suffers. Certainly, the collaboration among people required to resolve critical problems as they arise is not furthered by some human predilections: our desire to retain complete freedom in our personal attitudes and actions, a reluctance to join with unfamiliar people, an innate questioning of other people's motives, or concern about the uncertain consequences of cooperative action. Collaboration is made more difficult by the increasing substantive and operating complexities of civilization and the explosive population growth during the past century, which have aggravated disruptive religious differences, conflicting customs, tribal and group animosities, severe disparities of wealth and income, and political antagonisms.

There are further characteristics that set people apart. With few exceptions, other animals kill only for the food required to survive, to defend themselves against attack, or to effect evolutionary improvement of the species. The lion taking over an existing pride kills the cubs sired by the lion he drives away, and produces his own genetically superior offspring from the lionesses who acknowledged his dominance by becoming immediately sexually receptive. Benign survival of the fittest may lie behind the many wives of a tribal chief, but murder or genocide to attain privileged status is condemned when practiced and rarely acknowledged by civilized society. It is difficult to reason that modern wars promote natural selection. Humans are unique in their willingness to deliberately murder another member of their own species without defensive or evolutionary reason. With and without justification, humans harbor the conscious emotion of hate, absent in other animals. When we do not want to face the reality of our own inadequacy, or there is no individual or single group that can be held responsible, we almost always seek a scapegoat to blame, to hate, or to destroy in order to relieve a related or an unrelated emotion of our own.

Throughout history humans have been capable of deliberate cruelty, unknown in other animal species: torture; disfigurement and dismemberment; crucifixion; burning at the stake, within a flaming "tire necklace," or doused with gasoline; and other violent acts calculated to terrorize. Except for several insect societies, only humans enslave members of their own species, and they are the only animals that provide a low level of existence and security for a substantial portion of the population. Only humans foul their environment to the extent it causes sickness and death. Civilized man is materially acquisitive beyond his physical but not his emotional needs. In some individuals this is linked with a drive for personal power: manifest in a proportion of the population, successful leaders in society, powers behind the throne, and others exerting an inordinate influence. Certainly, lust for power lies behind the careers of many of the rulers who have shaped societies throughout history. It is difficult to imagine how these negative attributes could combine, cancel each other out, or otherwise function so as to favor the survival and advancement of the human species.

A degree of corruption is so common and widespread in human affairs that it should be considered a characteristic of human behavior, one which serves certain purposes but adversely affects individual character and the moral and legal improvement of society. Fundamentally, corruption is the consequence of the different motives of people. One person pays surreptitiously to obtain an advantage over others or to obtain the treatment he desires. People accept gratuitous payments to augment their income or because their position in society leads them to expect such pre- or post-payments for performing their duties. There are many human activities that incorporate this presumption, such as the invocation of favorable auguries or the removal of magical taboos, religious sanctions and prohibitions or the certification by inspectors and supervisors required at successive stages of construction, manufacturing, and many other operations.

> A broader explanation for the corruption, especially at the higher levels, is that in a modest economy, politics provides more certain access to wealth than business does. . . . It is also why those in power do not want to open up the system . . . it would mean allowing others to have a chance at that power and the money that goes with it—or to relax controls on the press and on speech, and thus risk being exposed.[1]

Commercial organizations supply products and services needed and desired by individuals and required for human affairs to function. Religious bodies render forgiveness from sins and spiritual succor. These actions are subject to preferential treatment which can prevent, delay, or alter human activities. They can produce or facilitate success. Or they can disappoint or inconvenience, cause financial hardship or economic ruin, abandonment of an activity or intention.

There is often an undesignated price to pay for the product or service that is officially provided without any special inducement or reward. It may be a bribe "under the table," a political "contribution," promise of a reciprocal favor, a "gift," a "tip," penance, or indulgence. In some countries the payment is an accepted cost of "doing business." It is considered neither immoral nor illegal. The extra payment is an acknowledgment of a favorable act, a proper means of supplementing personal income, a way of "sharing the wealth," or justified because it causes bureaucracies to perform when otherwise they would not. At times under certain conditions corruption may be necessary for people to survive. Gratuities, payoffs, bribes, and compensatory gifts are part of a spectrum of actions extending from an expression of appreciation for a service rendered to outright extortion. Actions of this nature are acceptable when they are the prevailing practice in some countries. They constitute corruption when they are exceptional, morally unacceptable, or illegal.

Individual characteristics that favor human advancement and survival are the obverse of or "counter" to the negative traits noted above: interest in and concern for others rather than selfish self-interest, love of other human beings rather than disdain, antagonism, or hostility that can escalate into hate. Open-mindedness or at least tolerance of other people with different customs or views, rather than preconceived prejudice. There are people who recognize and accept unpleasant realities as well as those who deceive themselves with unjustified optimism or wishful thinking. There are people who critically evaluate rather than automatically accept the implied validity of information presented in the mass media of communication, transmitted by word of mouth, circulated as rumor, or otherwise disseminated. Humans can react with sensory restraint as well as enjoying the pleasurable feelings of purely emotional response. They can be peaceably as well as hostilely inclined. They can take the longer-range view, look to and have a care for the future, or they can focus on the past and present only. The normal response of individuals to matters in general can be thoughtful and rational as well as disposed to provide emotional satisfaction. People can act wisely as well as stupidly. They can give as well as receive, act honestly as well as corruptly. And most do.

It is the positive potential of human character that has been the focus of prophets and religious institutions, and other organizations concerned with ethical and lawful behavior. Although it is anybody's guess, the great majority of the more than 5 billion people on earth probably react and act more in accordance with the positive than the negative characteristics of their species, since positive traits favor collective harmony and reduce societal discord. Insofar as we know from the few remaining examples of primitive people, they led peaceful lives for the most part, since this favors their individual well-being and their survival as a group. It appears as if the legend of Adam and Eve, the apple, and original sin does indeed represent the beginning of the negative characteristics of people, which have arisen during the advance of civilization. Most individuals exhibit both positive and negative attributes. The struggle continues between good and bad, virtue and vice, constructive and disruptive attitudes and actions.

SOCIETAL CHARACTERISTICS

On the one hand, the attributes of individuals all together form the fundamental features and determine the basic behavior of human groups, societies, and species. On the other hand, the survival of these collective entities requires certain behavior by their individual members. This mutual interdependence and accommodation are established over time by biological evolution in all animal species except man, who has greatly increased over the past several hundred years his unique capability to consciously affect his own individual and societal development and future.

Social insects are the supreme example of a binding relationship between individuals and the collective entity they comprise. Ants, termites, and bees "epitomize this kind of community in which several generations overlap, and individuals are divided into specialized castes that cooperate in producing and raising the young."[2]

> Different groups of the thousands of bees produced by the queen perform different activities: defending the entrance to the hive from intruders, keeping the hive clean, disposing of dead bees, controlling harmful parasites and pathogens, fanning the air with their wings to regulate its temperature and humidity, attending to the queen's bodily needs, and fertilizing the queen high in the air during her nuptial flight.[3]

Termites and ants have the same kind of rigid caste system in which the individuals in each specialized group are identical for all practical purposes, acting in the same way to perform a particular function in the collective life of the insect society. Individual and group behavior have been matched with each other and with the environment over millions of years of evolutionary development to ensure the survival of most animate species, insofar as this can be accomplished by adaptive adjustments. During the past several hundred thousand years, the evolutionary development of humanoids has been far faster than for other animate life. During the past several hundred years the rate of change brought about by Homo sapiens for himself and the world has increased. To avoid a prolonged period of individual stress and societal distress, humans have had to adapt not only to the forces of nature but also to the consequences of their own intellectual advancement, technological achievements, and diverse activities affecting local, regional, and global environments.

Each society and group of animals within a species has developed over time a combination of individual and group behavior favoring its survival. Some are tight-knit living in close contact within relatively small spatial habitats. The members of other groups range far and wide over great geographical distances, gathering at a propitious time to mate, reproduce, and begin another cycle of existence. Each group is a symbiotic integration of the individual and the collective entity. They have several character-istics in common: purposiveness, cohesiveness, and adaptability. Survival is the purposive or directive force. It requires cohesive actions among members of the group, and the capability of individuals separately and the group collectively to adapt to changing environmental conditions. Individuals communicate by sound, sight, odor, motion, vibration, color, and probably other mechanisms not yet identified by humans. Recent research concerning dolphins, whales, and elephants suggests that com-munication between some animals may be so expressive that it constitutes a rudimentary language. Actions by members of the group support the successful functioning of the whole in its purpose of collective survival and individual well-being. No member acts to prevent or impair this ob-jective.

The size of animal populations other than humans adjusts to the avail-ability of the food and water needed to propagate and survive, the effects of predators or competitors, and environmental conditions. Population size is directly related to the territory it must occupy for food. When there are too many, the population is reduced by attrition or by some of its members founding a new colony elsewhere. With some exceptions, conflicts among wild animals are ritualistic: peacefully establishing a hi-erarchy among individuals that determines the dominant male who will be the primary procreator, thereby favoring the evolutionary process of natural selection. This replaces the caste system of insect societies. Rarely do these conflicts result in serious injury or death. Some animal species support individual members of their group who are in trouble. All take deliberate action to protect and nurture the young as required for their well-being and survival. The activities of individuals are cohesive, co-operative, and mutually supportive in the best interest of the group and species. There is no willful aggression, violence, or deliberate cruelty among animals other than humans. They kill only when required for food, in self-defense, to protect the young, or to perpetuate the species. They are constantly alert to the environment on which their current condition and future depends.

Homo sapiens shares the instinct for survival with other animals, but it is most active and apparent in emergency situations rather than as an ever-present directive force. There are the basic human purposes of pro-creation, fulfillment of family needs, material gain, influence over other people, and other personal satisfactions. Each individual has specific ob-jectives particular to his needs, interests, and concerns. Rarely except in emergencies do large numbers of people act in concert with a common objective. So far in recorded history the human species has never acted cohesively as a whole with a single intent. In general, the history of human endeavors reflects the difficulties of attaining consistent action among many people. Humans share the adaptability of other animals, modifying their behavior to attain particular objectives but rarely because of the effects of their actions on the environment. During the past several hundred years of rapid population growth, humans have acted in many ways as if there were no limit to natural resources or the earth's capacity to absorb any and all human activities without serious environmental damage. Human beings are more diverse than the members of other animal species, and the human species is probably equalled in size by a number of insect species.

Since farming began, cultural evolution has gradually transformed Homo sapiens from a species evolving in response to a natural environment into one that is literally "making" the world in which it lives. After many millions of years living in groups of dozens or hundreds, in a mere ten millennia people have changed the world so much that they must now adjust to living in a "group" of 5 billion (since a global community is emerging).[4]

Some of the characteristics of people are very different from those of other species of animals. Communication skills are far more advanced, although the existence of hundreds of different languages and thousands of dialects make intraspecies intercommunication and understanding among people more difficult. Fortunately, English appears to be spreading as a common language for the future. The actions of people as individuals do not support successful functioning of our species as a collective group to the same extent that the actions of other animals do. Only man can act stupidly with relation to his own survival and advancement, since evolutionary development has eliminated or minimized unconstructive collective behavior by individuals in other species. "Showing mental dullness" is the negative aspect of the superior mental capabilities of humans.

One of the consequences of the diversity found among large numbers of people is that there are individuals with different or opposing views on almost all matters. It would be fortunate for humanity if mortal wars between people resulting from opposing views were settled by the ritual combat of other animals which occasionally produce injury but rarely death. Humans would kill other humans only when attacked, and other animals only for food. Unlike other species, arbitrary aggression, unprovoked violence, and deliberate cruelty are latent in people, kept in partial check by the restrictions of civilized behavior. Humans also help members of their own species, who are not members of their family unit, more than other animals but rarely enough to significantly reduce aggregate want in society. This may be because there are more humans in need than animals in need in other species, and people probably deny help to others as often as they provide it.

Over twenty years ago, Arthur Koestler postulated that "man is an aberrant species, suffering from biological malfunction, a species-specific

disorder of behavior which sets it apart from all other animal species—
just as language, science and art set it apart in a positive sense. The
creativity and pathology of man are two sides of the same medal."[5] The
first of man's fundamental character flaws enabled him to engage in human
sacrifice in the past, and to continue to do so in modified form today.
"Instead of being dismissed as a sinister curiosity of the past, the universality and paranoid character of the ritual should be regarded as symptomatic."[6] It underlies two other character flaws of humans: the weakness
of our inhibitions against individually killing members of our own species;
and our willingness and recurrent desire to collectively wage war among
ourselves, to persecute and engage in genocide against fellow human
beings. No other species of animal acts in these ways. There is also the
"permanent, quasi-schizophrenic split between reason and emotion, between man's critical faculties and his irrational, affect-charged beliefs,"[7]
which makes it doubly difficult to apply factual conclusions and rational
decisions in situations where this is crucial. And finally there is the "striking, symptomatic disparity between the growth curves of technological
achievement on the one hand and ethical behavior on the other—or, to
put it differently, between the power of the intellect when applied to
mastering the environment, and its impotence when applied to the conduct
of human affairs."[8] Whether these human characteristics threaten our
success and survival as a species, as Koestler believed, cannot be determined at the present time. But the facts on which his concerns are based
cannot be denied, nor the possibility he suggests ignored.

During the past several hundred thousand years, Homo sapiens has
become increasingly distinct from all other animal species. He has expanded his conscious awareness of being alive, with a limited life span
and the certainty of death, of being part of a social group and larger
society. Man's mental capabilities have increased: his capacity to consciously use his memory, to reason and ruminate rationally, to anticipate,
to plan and execute activities to achieve a predetermined objective. This
expanded consciousness underlies the emergence of civilized society,
which in its turn may accentuate existing traits or generate new characteristics that will enable man to continue to advance civilization and at
the same time to cope with the problems and complexities it brings.

Together with the anatomical enlargement of his brain and advancements in his capacity to think and to know, man maintains the nervous
system bequeathed to him by his forebears as their primary means of
response to external events and environmental conditions, and the primary mechanism of their evolutionary advance. This system of autonomic
sensing in man remains relatively unchanged, although the need for intensive use of all its sensibilities has changed as man's conscious awareness has expanded. In primitive times, for example, his sense of smell
was constantly alert to detect dangers before they materialized into a

visible and immediate threat. Civilized man relies on his sense of smell for fewer purposes. Most people are aware of few odors; they have replaced this sense in part by increased awareness of sights and sounds.

Despite the intellectual advance of civilized man, he is susceptible to emotional overreaction: a residual perhaps of his distant ancestors' need to react instantly in a threatening situation, to "fight or flee." In everyday activities, immediate response results in decisions and actions that might be different if emotional reaction is balanced with rational consideration. Reflecting the instinctive reaction of our early progenitors, we prefer emotional response to careful thought and simplistic answers to problems requiring complicated solutions. The emotional and rational components of man are not yet sufficiently integrated to ensure constructive response to external events and the wise resolution of pressing problems. This can contribute to societal tragedies when people succumb to the charisma of powerful personalities, responding to their emotional message but with little thought to the societal implications of their oratory and what they portend.

Man always has had to function collectively, at least with his immediate family and with his extended family, clan, tribe, or community as required for the provision of food, water, shelter, and protection from predators. Rudimentary collaboration became more complicated as groups increased in size, production processes and social organizations progressed, more competitors and antagonists appeared, and religious and behavioral concerns multiplied. With the advent and advance of industrial civilization, the range of consideration broadened rapidly to match the increasing economic complexity of human affairs. For the family, providing food, water, and shelter now involves outside services of many kinds. Dwelling units are more complicated. There are many different activities and choices with respect to transportation, communication, and financial, medical, educational, and recreational matters. As familiar an installation in the modern community as a major highway involves choosing its location, route design, engineering, a projection of costs and benefits, financing, construction, traffic laws and regulations, operation and maintenance, environmental impacts, and social consequences. The different elements to be considered are not only numerous, but many of them are complicated requiring special knowledge.

Although universally practiced in various ways, cooperation does not come easily for individuals. Man is psychologically a "lonely island." Cooperation is engendered by necessity, self-interest, convenience, rallying around a cause. Necessity ranges from the absolute minimum requirements for individual and collective survival to the gratification of a shared desire. People can and do collaborate continually and effectively in a multitude of situations. For example, despite accidents and exceptions, traffic in a multilane urban arterial street is an impressive example of cooperative behavior by those using it. Otherwise, the system could not and would not function; operational gridlock would be immediate and lasting. On a much larger scale, the international commercial air transportation system linking over 150 countries requires close collaboration in aircraft manufacture, maintenance, scheduling, flight operations, communications, and regulatory practices. Social and religious operations of many kinds depend on the collaborative behavior of their members. The world is filled with products, projects, and societal activities that could not and would not exist without cooperation among people.

This is especially true in the United States today. As a highly industrialized nation of some 250 million people, its economic and societal life consists of almost an infinity of different activities conducted separately by individuals and groups of people, but tied together in a vast network of formal and informal interconnections. Collaboration is essential for such a system of interrelationships to function effectively. People have recognized this fact and acted accordingly in creating and expanding the system—but with one all-important exception. They have not confronted, decided what to do, and acted with respect to the paramount problems facing society discussed in the first chapter and noted in various connections throughout this book. This failure is most conspicuous at the topmost level of governmental decision making where our elected representatives are responsible for acting in the best interests of the entire population within their jurisdiction. But they have become so politically partisan and concentrate so exclusively on reelection that legislative leadership and action in the general public interest has all but disappeared, except in some local governments where elected representatives are under closer scrutiny. Legislatures allow and even promote living on borrowed time and borrowed money by repeatedly postponing action on critical problems needing immediate attention, for fear of voter dissatisfaction and rejection at the polls. Issues pivotal to the human future are disregarded or treated superficially: such as the conservation and best use of natural resources; prevention, treatment, and disposal of different forms of waste and pollution; provision of affordable housing and shelter; or restricting expenditures to what the societal unit can afford currently or can foresee with certainty in the future.

One impediment to attaining the collaboration necessary to first prevent and then resolve such fundamental problems is rooted in U.S. history. Our nation was founded by people who wanted individual freedom that was not available to them in their country of origin. The United States was formed from thirteen separate colonies, with actual or potential differences so definite that they led less than ninety years later to civil war. These differences continue today on many matters vital to the nation as a whole. They are in part an outgrowth of the supreme importance attributed from the beginning to individual human rights and the constitutional rights of individual states. This emphasis has continued and even increased as attention has focused on minority rights and equal treatment. The rights of individuals have been expanded to now include freedom from bondage, want, and fear, freedom of expression and religious choice, and the right to privacy and equal opportunity. Individual rights have been expanded to include various organizations and activities. Religious groups believe that they have the right to practice their faith unrestricted in any way. The press cherishes its right to write what it wants and not to reveal its sources. Physicians and lawyers retain the right to keep confidential their work with patients and clients. Business enterprises claim that restriction on their activities violate their right to operate freely.

What has not received comparable attention during this period of emphasis on individual human rights are the rights of the societal group and species to function successfully and to survive as a collective entity. The two rights are interdependent since one cannot exist without the other. But they are not the same. For example, the social group must be able to prevent internal discord or redefine the individual rights of its members if either makes it impossible for the unit to exist and function. It must have the right to require longer-range considerations in planning and management since normally the group, community, or species has a longer life than its individual members. Many of the primary problems in the United States today would not exist or would be much less severe had the collective interest of society been considered in the past. Individual and group rights should be balanced for both to prosper and endure. This we have yet to accomplish in the United States and in most other countries in the world as well.

> At the individual level, people have begun to respond to increased awareness of global environmental change by altering their values, beliefs and actions. Changes in individual behavior are surely necessary but are not enough. It is as a global species—pooling our knowledge, coordinating our actions and sharing what the planet has to offer—that we have any prospect for managing the planet's transformation along pathways of sustainable development.[9]

Human collaboration is being put to the test by the continuing advances in scientific knowledge and technological development that call for positive response and greater cooperative action. Processes, products, and installations will become increasingly complex. Developments of many kinds, which we cannot envision today, will be achieved in the future. New means of transportation and communication will further transform the world. Instruments of violence and war will be more widespread and more destructive than ever. Biological manipulation and genetic engineering are in their infancy. New processes of rational analysis will be discovered. The rapidity and extent of scientific and technological advance pose a problem affecting everything and everyone on earth. It is a force in itself so powerful and pervasive—and with such momentum—that it constitutes a man-made and man-induced form of evolutionary development distinct from the chemical and biological evolution that has been going on for billions of years. Each of these two evolutionary forces exploits a different set of human characteristics affecting human reactions and responsive behavior. Will they function together constructively or destructively among the multitudinous members of the species Homo sapiens inhabiting very different geographical environments around the world, with diverse backgrounds, beliefs, customs, languages, educations, physical appearances, and economic conditions? Society seems to be finding it increasingly difficult to tap the human characteristics needed for constructive collaboration at the topmost level of decision making, or to inculcate in the young the positive response and sense of responsibility which they can apply when they are old enough to support or participate in such collaboration.

> Since 1900, the number of people inhabiting the earth has multiplied more than three times. The world economy has expanded 20 times. The consumption of fossil fuels has grown by a factor of 30, and industrial production has increased by a factor of 50; four-fifths of that increase has occurred since 1950. This scale of development has produced a world with new realities, realities that have not yet been reflected in human behavior, economics, politics or institutions of government.[10]

Of the more than 5 billion people in the world, approximately two-thirds are poor; about one-half have an annual income of less than U.S. $600, are homeless, or live in substandard housing, are without adequate, safe drinking water, and are illiterate; one-third are hungry and malnourished; 1 percent have a college education; 6 percent are Americans holding one-third of the world income. This is the nature, extent, and severity of the problems facing the human species today.

REFERENCES

1. Bonner, Raymond, "African Democracy," *New Yorker*, 3 September 1990, p. 103.
2. Koules, Bettyann, "The Ants," *Los Angeles Times*, 22 April 1990, p. 1.
3. Branch, Melville C., *Planning: Universal Process* (New York: Praeger, 1990), pp. 4–5.
4. Ornstein, Robert, and Paul Ehrlich, *New World, New Mind* (New York: Doubleday, 1989), p. 42.
5. Koestler, Arthur, "Man—One of Evolution's Mistakes?," *New York Times Magazine*, 19 October 1969, p. 28.
6. Ibid., p. 31.

7. Ibid.
8. Ibid., pp. 31, 108.
9. Clark, William C., "Managing Planet Earth," *Scientific American*, September 1989, p. 47.
10. MacNeill, Jim, "Strategies for Sustainable Economic Life," *Scientific American*, September 1989, p. 155.

3

SOCIETAL FEATURES AFFECTING PLANNING

If an agency is to have a sense of mission, if constraints are to be minimized, if authority is to be decentralized, if officials are to be judged on the outputs they produce rather than the inputs they consume, then legislators, judges, and lobbyists will have to act against their own interests. They will have to say "no" to influential constituents, forego the opportunity to expand their own influence, and take seriously the task of judging the organizational feasibility as well as the political popularity of a proposed new program.

James Q. Wilson
*Bureaucracy: What Government Agencies
Do and Why They Do It* (1989)

Planning is a universal process inherent in all human affairs. The kind of planning applied is determined by a society's stage of socioeconomic, scientific, and technological development, its political and economic systems, and its culture. Since these features vary widely among nations at any given time, and change with the passage of time, the planning practiced changes accordingly. Among the many societal characteristics that affect the conduct of planning, those discussed in this chapter refer to the situation in the United States at the end of the twentieth century. They may also apply to other countries with comparable societal characteristics, now or at some time in the future.

COMPLICATION

The progressive complication of human affairs makes planning more difficult. An increasing population burdens planning because the essential needs of additional people must be taken care of and their attitudes and desires taken into account. Life in industrialized countries becomes more complex as scientific and technical advances are applied to every element and at all levels of society. There are more people, more components, and many more interrelationships. Systems of communication, transportation, production, supply and distribution, economic and financial transactions, recreation and entertainment, and all others become more technically sophisticated and fine-tuned requiring a higher level of expertise in their design, manufacture, installation, operation, and eventual replacement. Many are subject to rapid obsolescence, replaced at shorter and shorter intervals with new or improved systems incorporating new technology.

These developments make planning analysis more complex and difficult, even with the progressive advances we have come to expect in the data processing and calculative capabilities of electronic computers. This difficulty may be reduced somewhat if artificial intelligence can perform some of the routine analysis involved in planning in a manner that produces results equivalent to those reached by a successful human analyst. The more complicated the planning, the more difficult it is for those formulating specific plans to conduct accurate analysis and reach sound conclusions. It also makes it next to impossible for those affected by plans to evaluate their quality, since the analysis employed is comprehensible to fewer and fewer people. One must therefore judge the value of plans by the results. But this can be misleading because the favorable or unfavorable situation when the plan is implemented may not be attributable to the plan alone; other factors may be responsible. We are obliged by the particular knowledge required to formulate plans and make decisions based on them, to have confidence in the work of those who can successfully perform this essential function in modern society.

Social insects create and accept automatically the crucial role of the queen bee, termite, or ant in the "planning" involved in their society and its evolutionary survival. In dictatorships with a single supreme leader— glorified with his portrait displayed in every public place, office, and home—the society functions like a completely regimented insect community. Except in centrally controlled societies, there are ways of reducing the negative aspects of the difference in knowledge between the managerial level and the public at large. The populace can establish if it so desires the overall purpose, general direction, public policies, and acceptable operational practices of the society. The specifics of formulating plans, making related decisions, and effectuating the plan are left to designated representatives, who can inform those concerned of the type of analysis employed and explain how and why certain key decisions were made. Allowing people to participate in this fashion goes a long way toward establishing the necessary confidence in the leadership. The genuineness of this participatory effort is crucial in a democracy, because it can be used by the leadership to misinform and manipulate the public as well as to accurately inform and obtain its support. As discussed in Chapter 4, the mass media of communication have a critical role in establishing and maintaining a constructive relationship between those who do the planning and the public which is the intended beneficiary.

As the process of planning becomes more complex it requires well-educated people to formulate and implement specific plans. For example, only those with special knowledge can understand the particular analysis supporting the planning required to manufacturer a new model automobile, to revise insurance practices or a tax code, or to improve mail service. Even those whom the plan affects most directly and those involved in implementing it must accept or reject the analysis behind it on faith. They may have confidence in the competence and integrity of those who prepare the plan. They may reject it out of hand because they are unwilling to accept a plan they cannot comprehend in every respect. Or they may concoct some other reason because they are reluctant to admit to themselves much less to others that they cannot comprehend something they think they should be able to understand. "The biggest barriers in getting people to buy insurance is overcoming their concern that insurance is complicated and confusing and therefore they run the risk of someone putting something over on them. . . . Research has shown that most people find insurance hard to understand."[1] The public at large cannot and does not attempt to fathom the science and engineering involved in most project plans. Nor do people aspire to such knowledge. Preoccupation with the tasks of daily life and realization of the education required preclude such concern.

As civilization progresses, the gap in knowledge widens between the few who conduct the analysis and those who make the decisions in planning, and the many who are affected. The public in general and most individuals affected by particular plans must accept on faith those portions requiring special knowledge. Relatively few plans, however, contain essential content that only a few people can comprehend and evaluate. And usually such technical matter does not involve the most important considerations represented in the primary elements of the plan. In those cases where technical aspects are "of the essence," plans can be evaluated by a group of qualified individuals other than those who prepared the plan, or they must be judged by the outcome.

THE CHANGING SCENE

The profound effects of advances in science and technology are evident on all sides. The most potentially impactful of these are certainly the destructive weapons developed in less than fifty years: nuclear explosives, intercontinental ballistic and other types of aimed and guided missiles, highly toxic chemical weapons and deadly nerve gases, and increasingly destructive aircraft, ground weapons, and military naval vessels. Ballistic missiles with their multiple-targeted nuclear warheads can be delivered within an hour almost anywhere in the world, the bomb and missile loads of military aircraft in a matter of hours, troops within days, naval vessels within weeks. More and more countries are acquiring nuclear and other destructive capabilities. Most seek military power and intend to get it one way or another. Many are in the business of manufacturing and selling sophisticated weapons. There appears to be no limit to continued increase in the military capabilities of nations around the world. And the nature of modern military systems is such that a single deliberate or inadvertent act could trigger an international or regional holocaust. The situation is loaded with imminent danger and potential destruction for large numbers of the human species.

Science has made possible almost instantaneous communication connecting most parts of the world. Faster forms of transportation facilitate frequent travel and the shipment of goods far and wide as never before. These developments have linked monetary exchange, financial, manufacturing, political, and recreational activities—once largely separated in time and space—into a global network of close interconnection. "Summit" meetings and communication by telephone "hot lines" among political leaders, personal visits by government officials, and working conferences between government personnel occur with increasing frequency. The speed and volume of transactions among the financial and commodity markets around the world are many times greater than they were not long ago. Transactions that took weeks or months are now completed in far shorter times. Fast transport of raw materials, commodities, finished products, and unfinished goods among the nations of the world has vastly expanded. These capabilities of immediate communication and fast transportation have promoted the internationalization of manufacturing operations—once contained with few exceptions within national boundaries—to locations around the world where labor rates or other conditions are most favorable.

> Capital investment in overseas operations that are at least 50 percent owned by American companies rose 13 percent in 1989, and an additional 17 percent in 1990. . . . Many companies are also putting operations abroad to take advantage of low wages for skilled labor. And finally, overseas profitability is often much higher than in the United States.[2]

As discussed in the next chapter, the mass media of communication have transformed the people of the world into one enormous audience: receiving information and reacting continually all together and almost at the same time to the same world events and problems as they are presented in each country by newspapers, radio, periodicals, and—above all—television.

Scientific and technological developments have introduced new inter-relationships and new interdependencies among nations. A society living in isolation or functioning independently of the rest of the world is no longer possible. The new network of interaction produces rapid reaction. It ingests and disseminates an enormous volume of diverse information. It is subject to rumor, speculation, distortion, and political manipulation. Since it reaches into most dwellings and workplaces throughout the world, it magnifies the effects of whatever it presents by the magnitude and universality of the exposure. It can impress by repetition. Unfortunately, electromagnetic communication systems employing computers are technically vulnerable to criminal use and malicious disruption. Altogether, the characteristics of the global communication and transportation systems call for a high level of continuous planning with respect to their employment and operational maintenance.

Together with population growth and the added economic requirements it imposes, industrial technology is responsible for the world's major environmental problems. Global warming and ozone depletion are the result of burning fossil fuels in industrial processes and machines. After years of irresolution, the United States has not yet decided how to store safely the growing accumulation of intensely radioactive waste with a half-life of hundreds of years—a physical material that did not exist in volume fifty years ago. "Radioactive waste, it would seem, remains an issue too hot to handle."[3] It also remains to be seen whether existing operating and evacuation plans will reduce the danger of fatalities, injuries, and damage from nuclear accidents, such as occurred in 1986 at the Chernobyl electric power generating plant in the Soviet Union. The consequences of this single accident, caused by "human error," have come to light only gradually through the screen of government censorship. At least several thousand people were killed quickly by fatal radiation. An area of 125,000 square kilometers was rendered uninhabitable, including a new town of 60,000 people. Some 3 million people in the surrounding countryside were exposed to injurious radiation, which only now after five years is producing abnormal ailments in the living and birth defects in the newborn. The economic loss is calculated at $350 billion or more. And all of this by a form of contamination undetectable by the human senses. There are now, in 1992, 431 nuclear power plants in 25 nations.

Disposal, recycling, and reduction of the enormous quantities of industrial and household waste produced in the United States—more than in any other country—have hardly begun. Disposal of toxic waste is so far behind the amounts produced that it is being sold and shipped for further use in developing nations, although it is known that they have no means of safely processing the material and disposing of the residue. Besides adding to global contamination, this dumping of hazardous waste in poorer countries where it imperils human health is regarded by some people as irresponsible if not immoral behavior by the United States—an example of the unexpected effects and ramifications of environmental problems. Chemicals have been allowed to seep into the ground in many places, contaminating water wells and endangering underground aquifers that provide potable water for many people.

> From 1986 to 1988, 24 states and Puerto Rico reported 26,000 illnesses linked to contaminated drinking water. . . . Another report, released by the [U.S. Environmental Protection Agency] in 1987, found that from 1971 to 1985, there were 111,228 reported cases of diseases caused by consumption of contaminated drinking water. . . . Some researchers believe that the actual number of waterborne diseases from drinking water may be 25 times the reported incidence.[4]

Most recently, it has been found that "physically undetectable [electromagnetic] fields can produce physiological and behavioral changes. So far, however, none of these whole-body changes have been linked to specific health effects."[5] It is clear that a great deal of planning must be accomplished before the environmental consequences of civilization can be managed safely.

The repercussive effects of scientific advances are nowhere more apparent than in medicine. New pharmaceuticals are developed in a seemingly never-ending stream. Surgical procedures that were new not long ago are now common practice: open-heart, vascular, corneal, arthroscopic. Prosthesis is now available for every major joint except the shoulder, which undoubtedly will be forthcoming before long. Highly sophisticated diagnostic equipment has been created: computer tomographic scanning, magnetic resonance imaging, fiberscopic endoscopic viewing. Genetic and other biological interventions are just beginning. Such dramatic developments produce a new set of problems concerning medical practice and medical care. For example: the extent to which support systems should be used to maintain autonomous reactions in irreversibily comatose or brain-dead patients, or intensive care to prolong the "life" of the terminally ill close to death; inequities in the availability of some medical treatment because of its high cost; the nature and extent of universal medical care; the optimum division of research expenditures between prevention and cure.

Such considerations brought to the fore in medicine call attention to the all-encompassing and most fundamental question that scientific and technical advance poses for human society as a whole. Can we cope with the momentous changes and challenges to our societal existence brought about continually by science and technology? Can we avoid destroying a substantial portion of our species with the ever more deadly arsenal of destructive weapons available to more and more nations? Can we act in worldwide and regional concert to prevent environmental contamination that injures and kills people, and avoid environmental catastrophe that could pollute our planet for generations and threaten our survival? Can we avoid the societally destructive consequences of the ever-increasing disparity between the haves and the have-nots, the possibility of an uprising by the disadvantaged resulting in a period of violent worldwide conflict and societal chaos that sets back civilization for a long time?

Or does science and technology constitute a new form of evolution, so powerful in itself that it shapes our future and affects the physical features of the earth? Will it effect such change that human society can no longer cope with the consequences and destroys itself or gradually disintegrates? Or will science and technology act as a constructive element of evolution that compels the human species to overcome its difficulties of individual and collaborative behavior and engage in a collective effort to advance civilization and preserve our planet and our species?

SHORT-TERM VERSUS LONG-RANGE

Early man was intuitively concerned above all else with survival, and therefore with the immediate present, which required instantaneous reaction to sudden threats to himself and his family. The necessity of considering the environment extended his range of perception and action to seasonal and other changes over time that affected his obtaining food and shelter. Efforts to propitiate the gods were directed toward favorable supernatural response in the future. Early evolutionary development and most recently civilization have progressively increased people's involvement with the future as their activities have become more complicated, requiring careful planning and longer and longer times to complete many endeavors. Individuals who acquired some surplus means could spend it for something they desired in the future. In general, individuals look ahead to the extent they find it is necessary or desirable to consider the future. For informal groups and formal organizations, looking ahead relates to the complexity and economic condition of the society as well as to individual attitudes. Most people do not like to speculate about the future; they recall how often they have been wrong when they attempted to do so. And they are reluctant to accept long-range projections because their fulfillment requires consistent human behavior, which they have observed is rarely maintained for long. Some people believe that looking ahead and planning are useless and undesirable since the future is preordained by divine will and intervention.

Although they are well aware of the necessity or desirability of taking action with respect to the future, elected officials avoid doing so to the extent possible. They fear that a commitment or even an implied approval of a longer-range objective, which their constituency favors at the time, may backfire later when conditions, public attitudes, and specific priorities have changed. The public can change its mind about a planning policy or its support of a particular plan at any time, forgetting or ignoring its previous concurrence. Or the elected official may be held responsible for the failure or only partial success of a planning program that he neither formulated nor specifically approved, due to adverse developments no one could anticipate. All too often responsibility is assigned by inference or because of the need for a scapegoat. In recent years the American public has been so conditioned to seek and accept services and benefits that must be paid for in the future that any reduction in what is currently available is regarded as an unacceptable deprivation. Immediate gratification for the living is the order of the day.

"The problem is that the costs of solving our basic problems will come in the short term while the advantages would come only after the end of every current officeholder's term of office. So it's in no one's political interest to force us to start paying the price now."[6] As a consequence, most elected officials swing and sway with the attitudes and desires of their constituency at the moment, avoiding plans or commitments that might backfire in the future at election time. Better safe than sorry. This has resulted in "management by crisis," which is now characteristic of most governments in the United States. Failure to act on primary problems until they become so severe they can no longer be deferred ensures the socioeconomic collapse that is fast approaching.

> Had the politicians faced the reality of the [savings and loan fiasco] in 1982, it would have cost $20 billion; in 1984, the costs had doubled to $40 billion; in 1988–89, they more than doubled again. Now, we are looking at between $500 billion and $1 trillion, not including the untold tens of billions we will all pay indirectly through generally higher interest rates. . . . This kind of defer-problems-at-all-costs approach will cost everyone about $2,500 in taxes or foregone government services.[7]

"Politicians and voters seem unwilling to address . . . larger issues especially if suggested cures seem to carry large price tags with no guarantees. They prefer instead to concentrate on more immediate symptoms and dramatic, seemingly simple solutions."[8]

Reluctance to commit to the longer-range future also exists in business in the United States, where success is judged by short-term performance, reported in quarterly accounting statements. If the "bottom line" is not favorable, corporate prospects are discounted. Resources are concentrated on the near term, with insufficient allocation for continuing research, development, and preparation for the production of new or improved products or services in the future. Executives are especially fearful of commitments that may be desirable or even necessary but will take years to execute. This investment in the future reduces current profits in favor of higher average returns over a longer period of the company's life; it could jeopardize an executive's salary bonus, stock options, or even his job. Overemphasis on the "bottom line" showing short-term profit satisfies the current criterion of success, but it also can lead to business failure. Some observers believe that it is the insistence by lending institutions and other investors in the United States on current profits that accounts for the failure of many American companies to compete successfully with their Japanese counterparts who plan and manage for the longer range.

MARKETS, PLANNING, AND PRIVATE ENTERPRISE

Except for nations with completely centralized economies, markets are part of the economic system, places where many kinds of possessions and rights are bought and sold. Even in the most highly controlled economies "black markets" exist, as attested by their name. Trading, bartering, buying, and selling among people is a basic activity that can be suppressed but not eliminated.

A distinction often is made between planned and so-called unplanned market economies: one implying rigid economic control, the other free exchange among people of whatever they want to exchange. This is a common misstatement because planning is necessarily involved both in the choice between the two economic systems and in the conduct of both. As a universal process, planning does not start or stop according to the type of economy or the extent of market activity. It is explicit or implicit in both. In government-directed economies planning is explicit and its effects on the functioning of the society apparent to all. Planning in market economies is explicit in the choice to have them, and implicit in their self-directed or government-supervised operations. Markets cannot function effectively in complete chaos; at least a minimum degree of organization must be established intentionally or emerge from a process of trial and error.

In the United States, discussion of markets and planning is really about a more basic underlying question: What are the respective roles of government and private enterprise in a society? Markets exist in some form in every country—for example, as areas of potential sales in free societies or places where products produced by government are offered for sale in centrally planned societies. The respective roles of government and private enterprise vary widely, of course, among nations. In Austria all of the basic economic activities are owned and operated by the state: postal service; telecommunications; the production and distribution of electricity, natural gas, oil, and coal; railroads and airlines; steel-making and automobile manufacture. In the United States seven of these basic economic activities are owned and operated by private enterprise under government regulation, as are also three-quarters of the nation's electrical system, railroads and some postal services.

Both countries plan and function successfully under their very different political philosophies and ownership preferences. Which system meets the needs and desires of people most successfully depends on the respective capabilities of government and business, and whether the nation benefits most from a preponderance of public or private institutions, or a combination of both. In any case it is government as the sovereign power that is ultimately responsible for the functioning of the society. For example, were private enterprise to fail completely in one of the societal functions it performs in the United States—such as the systems of communication or manufacture—the government would have to step in and operate them.

Certain functions in a society must be established and maintained by the sovereign government: the nature of the law of the land and the means and methods of ensuring order, the extent of public and private ownership, the degree of freedom of expression and affiliation, the monetary and communication systems, the military establishment. The government does not, however, have to be the operating agency for many of its responsibilities. In the United States: "A recent survey found city governments contracting out for at least 66 different services, ranging from refuse collection to planning and subdivision control."[9] Also, vouchers are used to pay private enterprises for various services such as the day care of children of working mothers and rent supplements.

> The forms of government action have not just become more numerous. In the process, an important transformation has occurred in the way government, especially the federal government, operates in the domestic sphere. In particular, many of the newer, or most rapidly growing tools of government action share a common characteristic: they are indirect, they rely upon a variety of non-federal "third parties"—states, cities, banks, industrial corporations, hospitals, non-profit organizations, etc.—for their operations.[10]

These developments accentuate age-old questions or raise new ones concerning the form and functioning of government and its contribution to people's current well-being, prospects, and survival. As a matter of political philosophy, do people want a government policy that maintains an overall proportionate relationship between the activities carried out by the governmental civil service and those performed for government by private enterprise? Does contracting out governmental activities to private enterprise produce superior results in the public interest for the same amount or less money?

> The profit motive and the need to control costs are absent in the non-competitive environment of public transit. . . . Competitive contracting is not an abdication of the public responsibility to ensure safe, efficient, and equitable service. The public transit agency retains full control of the service; the agency decides which services are provided, where and when they operate, and what fares are charged. . . . The public saves an average of 30% on competitively contracted routes.[11]

Is this a "private expropriation of public's authority" or a "public use of private interest"? How much discretionary authority is to be delegated? Can accountability be established and monitored so that the arrangement is not misused by not carrying out the public intent, by not meeting standards of operation, or by corruption? Does the proliferation of for-profit and nonprofit organizations performing delegated governmental activities make governance so complex that the overall direction and management of public affairs is necessarily less successful than it was when fewer elements were involved? Does it represent an abrogation of sovereignty or responsibility, an acknowledgment of inherent governmental incompetence, or the best way of conducting a wide range of activities?

Rather than delegating activities to private enterprise, should efforts be directed toward making civil service an efficient and effective force in the public interest? Is it possible to motivate, measure performance, and improve the professional status and the image of public employees so that governmental bureaucracies function as well as their counterparts in private enterprise? Is it ever justified to create a bureaucracy of competent people in government for political reasons in order to attain a loyalty comparable to that expected of employees in private organizations? Is it appropriate in some countries at certain times to use governmental bureaucracies to provide temporary employment and a constructive experience for those who would otherwise be unemployed, such as the Civilian Conservation Corps in the administration of President Franklin D. Roosevelt?

> America's most articulate conservative thinker proposes a plan for universal voluntary national service for men and women 18 years of age and older. . . . A nation can have "afflictions" that "are not registered in conventional supply-demand terms. . . . " One such affliction is the failure to acknowledge a running debt to one's homeland (biological or adopted). That is one deficiency that national service seeks to accost.[12]

Answers to these important questions concerning the administrative organization of their operations are rarely discussed publicly by the governments themselves. Their conclusions are to be seen in the form and functioning of their activities. Planning is involved in whatever mix of government and private enterprise is adopted. The belief that capitalism operates by unplanned market mechanisms, and that socialist societies are planned by comparison is a misconception. It fails to recognize the universality of planning. Many people accept this misunderstanding and assume that planning is not present or is undesirable in a market-oriented society, and that markets are not present in centralized or socialistic societies, which are planned. Although the particular purpose, content, and employment of planning are different in the two applications, the basic process of analysis and conclusion are the same.

LEGISLATIVE AND ADMINISTRATIVE DEADLOCK

As the number of people and the accumulation of knowledge increase at an almost exponential rate, there is a corresponding increase in the instruments of effectuation that direct society's activities. The technical content of science, technology, and engineering alone call for a vast documentation to carry out projects and indicate how things must be done to replicate results previously attained or to break new ground. There are a multitude of instruments of effectuation employed in the United States by government and private enterprises: laws, executive orders, directives, rules, regulations, requirements, conditions, standards, instructions. They require monitoring to ensure that the prescribed actions are taken.

The proliferation of laws enacted by the federal government, 50 states, approximately 3,000 counties, and several hundred thousand municipalities has produced a maze of legislated prescriptions and an almost impossible task of implementation and coordination. Many of these laws and more of the related requirements are inconsistent or contradictory, particularly at the local and state levels of governments. The American public has come to believe that "passing a law" will in itself solve any problem or achieve the desired result. Legislators are prone to make use of this belief. They can claim to have met their constituents' wishes if legislation is enacted that addresses the matter in mind, although the legislator knows it cannot produce the imputed result. Even when it is known that the proposed law has little chance of enactment, the legislator's claim to have made a valiant effort is usually enough to satisfy those concerned. "In the California legislature alone [in 1975] 7,000 bills were proposed."[13] Most laws are passed without due regard for the cost, administrative procedures, and related consequences of carrying them out. New government agencies add to the volume of laws and regulations. "More than 200 major federal agencies, bureaus, and commissions [were] created in [the fifteen-year period between 1960 and 1975]; only a handful have been abolished."[14] Most recently, a new set of eleven regional planning bodies was established in one state and regional governments are proposed in another.

A consequence of this increasing flood of directives is that it has become impossible to make sure that they are observed. Requirements and standards are pointless if they are not fulfilled. Many local ordinances in land-use planning incorporate actions that must be carried out subsequently as a condition of the grant. This requires follow-up inspection to make sure that the conditions imposed are met. Local health regulations prescribed by law require sanitary facilities, conditions, and practices in all commercial establishments where food is prepared and served to prevent food poisoning and the spread of infectious disease. Unannounced inspections determine if these are being honored. Every new building and remodeling requires a sequence of inspections to check if each step in construction is completed in accordance with the building and safety code before it is covered over by subsequent construction.

The success of the hundreds of thousands of such systems established in the public interest depends on voluntary compliance to ensure that the implementation and continued operation of many human activities are conducted safely for those affected. Without this conformance more inspectors would be required to regularly police these systems than are available in the work force. For example: "The [Environmental Protection Agency] acknowledges that the lack of resources has meant that the state and Federal officials take action in less than 2 percent of the thousands of complaints reported each year [concerning the quality of drinking water]."[15] Unfortunately, the situation with respect to legislated compliance, inspection, and control in the United States is deteriorating. Besides the sheer volume of rules and regulations, specific interpretation often is required at the site and inadvertent or deliberate misunderstandings occur too late to correct. The ethical values underlying voluntary compliance are being eroded by the disintegration of many family units, the creation of a socioeconomic underclass, and examples of corruption and lawlessness in high places reported in the mass media every day. Add to these influences the long-established American attitude that trying to "beat the system" is acceptable, that whatever "you can get away with" is all right. Also, people's awareness of and active concern for the public interest has been overshadowed by the emphasis on individual rights with far less regard for societal responsibilities.

ESTIMATION, PROJECTION, AND REALITY

Like most activities, successful planning depends on the accuracy of the information used to determine the sequence of actions that should produce the desired result. Significant error in the underlying data and the analysis based on it is apparent when the next step planned cannot be carried out because the real situation encountered is different from what was projected. If this occurs at an early stage in implementing the plan and it is not too all-encompassing, it is often possible to revise the plan rather than abandon it. If the error occurs when the plan is close to realization, a much larger investment of time, money, and human effort is at stake; a last-minute salvage is the best hope of cutting losses and realizing some part of the intended accomplishment. A plan inadvertently based on erroneous information is a delusion. One based on data known to be inaccurate is a fraud. In both cases, if correction is impossible, the project cannot be realized as planned and planning as a desirable process is likely to be discredited in the eyes of those involved. The consequences of such failures vary, of course, with the nature of the plan and its scope. Comprehensive plans covering all the principal elements of an organization that are based on inaccurate information cause the greatest internal procedural damage. Faulty plans affecting the fate and fortune of many people cause the greatest external damage.

Information may be imprecise because there are no precedents to support a more specific statistical statement. Certain methods of deriving information, such as public opinion polls and selective sampling of all kinds, produce results within a range of accuracy. Sufficient information may not exist to forecast political developments or the attitudes and behavior of people. Who would have predicted the actions of President Mikhail S. Gorbachev of the Soviet Union that led to his receiving the 1990 Nobel Peace Prize, the reunification of Germany, or the activities of President Saddam Hussein of Iraq—developments affecting operational planning by the countries involved and strategic planning by most nations around the world? Inaccurate information may be due to procedural errors in its collection or processing. Often data are made available without any indication of their range of probable error. They may be mishandled in analysis, or so simplified to make them mathematically tractable that they are no longer truly representative. Projections into the future and predictions of coming events contain their own uncertainties.

There are other causes of inaccuracies in planning of a different nature. To the extent possible most people minimize distressing news and disturbing developments. A hopeful attitude and optimistic expectations are more emotionally satisfying than pessimism and the discouragement of expecting the worse. We would like to avoid having to think about and act on worrisome problems. Even when we realize that the situation is critical and something must be done, we prefer to postpone action until it can be delayed no longer, until time passes and it becomes someone else's problem, or we hope that somehow it will disappear. This avoidance and wishful thinking makes effective planning difficult if not impossible. By definition, planning must identify and treat the primary problems of the organization or situation with which it is concerned, however severe and disheartening they may be. Successful decision makers cannot engage in unrealistic pretense and procrastination.

Another set of inaccuracies that may occur in planning involves underestimation, a human predilection far more widespread than generally recognized. We tend to project the costs of projects and programs, and the outcome of expected events, more favorably than justified by the facts. Most of the time the costs turn out to be much higher and the time required for completion much longer than estimated, and the consequences of unfavorable events much worse than forecast. It appears that we have built in within us a positive attitude and a hopeful outlook that are an important part of the sense of well-being we cherish and the motivation we need to face the trials and tribulations of human existence. To continuously acknowledge critical problems and absorb adverse circumstances in all their disturbing reality is more than most people can tolerate or are willing to accept—except in emergencies or after a prolonged period of consideration. Hope must spring eternal or be tempered gradually, but never abandoned completely.

Since informal groups and formal organizations are composed of individuals, they tend to misstate matters in the same way. There are executives known to be so overoptimistic that operating personnel routinely discount their forecasts to fit past and present realities. In general, subordinates seek to avoid negative or pessimistic reports to their superiors, sometimes to the extent of providing misleading information. Politicians may believe that if the public—or their fellow legislators—knew the true cost of a proposed program or project they would not approve it. The tactic of underestimating in order to get one's "foot in the door" is well known and widely practiced, and once engaged in it is not likely to be abandoned. There are also more and more instances of fraudulent misstatement, deliberate misrepresentation, and corruption that distort information. For example: "A giant hydroelectric power project [in Argentina] . . . has turned into a nightmare of delays and cost overruns that President Carlos Saul Meneem says make it 'a monument to corruption.'"[16]

Some 87% of managers in a National Association of Accountants study were willing to commit fraud in one or more of the cases presented to them. More than half were willing to overstate assets, while 48% said they would establish insufficient return reserves for defective products and 38% said they would pad a government contract.[17]

Serious criminal fraud had been discovered at 60% of the savings institutions seized by the government in 1989—triple the fraud rate in failures of commercial banks.[18]

The above report is particularly distressing because so many people rely on the accounting profession to review the accuracy of the financial affairs of individuals and the fiscal operations of organizations. If financial information descriptive of business organizations becomes generally inaccurate or dubious, a wide range of planning that utilizes these data is subject to consequent error. Are we on our way in the United States to the two sets of accounting records maintained in some countries, one for internal use only and the other with different information available to government and the outside world? Daily newspapers, television, and periodicals report the never-ending stream of inaccurate statements made by civil governments, businesses, the military services, and just about every type and size of organization, and by individuals in every walk of life. Several examples of the kind of inaccurate statements that erode public confidence will suffice to confirm the problem. The supreme example is probably the savings and loan debacle referred to previously in this chapter, a situation that has escalated from an initial cost of $20 billion to a forthcoming cost of between $500 billion and $1 trillion. In this and the several additional examples that follow, either those concerned could not accurately forecast at the time, refused to face and state the facts, or deliberately misrepresented the real situation.

Continuing economic fallout from the Chernobyl nuclear accident may cost 20 times Moscow's prior estimates.[19]

The U.S. Secretary of Energy reports that it will cost $6 billion for each of the next 5 years to clean up nuclear waste from 20 federal weapons plants, 50 percent more than estimated 6 months ago. The total cost could be $200 billion.[20]

The Central Design group of the [Superconducting Supercollider] completed its preliminary plans in 1986, estimating the overall cost of the machine at $5.9 billion. . . . The estimated cost now stands at nearly $8 billion.[21]

In the last two weeks, the Japanese Government has concluded that the cost of developing the plane has nearly doubled. . . . [It] will be so expensive and late that it will be nearly obsolete by the time the plane takes off.[22]

At the local level: "From a preliminary estimate of $30 million, the municipal Civic Center has grown in size and complexity to the point where the total cost may exceed $120 million, according to city officials' latest estimates."[23]

It is clear from the above indications that some of the information needed for sound planning is subject to inaccuracies that can affect the validity of plans, even though correct methods of analysis are employed. As noted, some of these inaccuracies are procedural in nature, and com-

pensating adjustments or replacement may be possible. Others are politically or personally self-seeking in nature, grossly underestimating the
true costs of an activity or otherwise disguising some other reality. If
human motivations to misstate costs and discount difficulties are as prevalent as they seem, perhaps indices of reality should be developed that
automatically increase early estimates by applying a multiplier.

EMOTIONS AND RATIONALITY

Planning is a rational process. As discussed in the previous section, it
seeks accurate information to support reliable analysis. By no means are
emotional or even irrational factors excluded from consideration in formulating plans. They may be included as elements in the plan if they are
important in the behavior of individuals or groups of people involved, or
in the functioning of the society as a whole. If plans are soundly conceived
and realizable, they deal with the real situation they address in all respects.
Objectives cannot be so vaguely stated that it is impossible to program
specific actions to achieve them. The resources available to carry out the
plan cannot be so exaggerated or illusory that the proposed endeavor is
a fiction. Nor can the analysis underlying the plan be so warped by unrealistic or partisan inputs that it is no longer valid. These requirements
have been brought to the fore by the advancements in the capability of
individuals and societies to plan ahead, which have come about in little
more than 200 years.

The adversarial system permeating most activities in the United States
assumes that confrontation and combative competition between oppo-
nents is the best way of determining leadership; governing the nation,
states, and localities; rendering justice; and attaining maximum business
efficiency. The extremes to which the competitive system can be carried
are becoming the rule rather than the exception. "Today's [political]
campaigns have become a kind of harrowing arms race, fueled by ever
more sophisticated technologies, waged with ever more brutal and efficient techniques, covering more and more personal and political terrain."[24] Periodically, legislatures and chief executive officials become
locked in budget battles extending well beyond established deadlines disrupting operations, sometimes threatening to shut down governmental
activities for want of appropriated funds. There are similar confrontations
at state and local levels of government. Judicial trials concerning relatively
unimportant social and legal issues are being drawn out for years in some
cases, at great public and private expense. For the ordinary citizen, the
time it takes to get on the court calendar is so long and the costs of the
prolonged wait so large that "justice delayed is justice denied." Few
people can afford to take a case to court. Adversarial excess is also
increasing in the business community. "In a stunning disclosure, Amer-

ican Express admitted last year that it had engaged in a covert campaign
to ruin Mr. Safra's reputation by spreading rumors and articles in the
international press . . . what its chairman, Mr. Robinson, called an 'un-
authorized and shameful effort.' ''[25] No other animal species operates
with the adversarial system, beyond the ritual confrontation or other
action which establishes a hierarchy of leadership and survival of the
fittest by selective procreation. Collaboration is the main mechanism of
societal existence and survival. Adversarial acts do occur between different species as nature's method of maintaining a balance between pre-
dator and prey.

Antagonistic actions are part of the politics to select among candidates
in the primary election, and then to choose the preferred person for the
office in a final election. Individuals seeking positions in private enterprise
and organizations selling products or services often are selected by competitive interviews. Although adversarial procedures can be employed for
various managerial purposes, plans to achieve designated objectives with
specific programs of action cannot be conceived, much less formulated
and implemented, as a series of adversarial confrontations. Resolution of
differences that affect the basic purpose and content of plans is achieved
before specific plans are drawn for the myriad projects and programs
undertaken by people all over the world every day—except at the top
levels of legislative leadership and decision making where personal and
partisan politics reign and rage in their most intensive and prolonged form.
When political and legal systems cannot each resolve their adversarial
excesses, successful planning is unlikely if not impossible.

Certain characteristics of people in general, together with the political
system in the United States as it has developed, make planning particularly
difficult at the highest level of governmental decision making where the
most critical actions affecting society are taken. The use of "labels" is
one of these. Rather than state specifically or describe carefully what we
have in mind, we resort to simplistic terms that permit a wide range of
interpretation. We use words such as conservative, liberal, reactionary,
activist, unscientific, democratic, progressive. They suggest different
things to different people; they can be used in different ways. People have
such diverse understanding of these labels, or they suggest such different
things in their minds, that they have little meaning in themselves. Yet
they can have great impact when delivered by prominent people, at the
right time, with great conviction. They can be used as weapons. Calling
someone any one of the illustrative labels above can be delivered as an
accusation or an epithet—or as a tribute or compliment. One need only
listen to political representatives when they arise to address their constituents on a controversial issue, on television, videotape, for the record,
or directly in person. Their impassioned oratory contains many more
labels and glittering generalities than meaningful statements. "Reading

between the lines" is usually a useless attempt to discover meaningful statement where none was intended.

Glittering generalities are expressions that almost certainly do not mean the same thing to the person making the statement, the person or persons addressed, and just about everybody else. "When someone talks to us about 'democracy,' we immediately think of our own definite ideas about democracy. . . . Our first and natural reaction is to assume that the speaker is using the word in our sense, that he believes as we do on this important subject."[26] We cannot know if this is the case from the use of the single word. Different people have different concepts of what democracy means in the way of freedoms, political, governmental, and legal systems, and other characteristics each person has in mind. The term must be amplified or explained to some degree to be more than an almost meaningless generality.

In recent years various expressions advocating "less government" have been widely and repeatedly used for political purposes. By employing a glittering generality calling for reduction in the size or scope of government the user satisfies and secures the support of those who believe he means what each of them has in mind. He may not know himself exactly what he has in mind, but he does not clarify his thoughts because he knows there are governmental functions of some sort that each person wants continued or even increased. When he is questioned, to avoid alienating the particular group and still retain his posture of advocating less government, he can claim or infer that he does not favor reducing the particular benefit or service the group does not want to be curtailed. He can change his disclaimer to fit different situations.

There are a multitude of such glittering generalities—expressions that have no significance in themselves, but nonetheless have high emotional appeal and political impact. They can be presented and interpreted as an indication of agreement, as a criticism, inducement, or adversarial weapon. They are by no means limited to politics but are employed at one time or another by most people. A deliberate effort is required when making certain statements to avoid the misunderstanding and confusion overgeneralizations can create.

Exaggeration is the overstatement of information or the intensified description of events that is part of many people's everyday conversation and most group discussions. It is our effort to make a point, or to express our strong feelings, which we believe would not be conveyed if we did not overemphasize. It reduces the need or necessity to be precise, which is more difficult conceptually and linguistically. We may need to clarify our own thoughts if this is required for us to be more accurate. Exaggeration enables us to be more dramatically articulate, to express ourselves more vigorously than usual, to defend or attack an issue or individual without having to be specific. We may believe that our expression is accurate rather than an overstatement. Or we can exaggerate as a deliberate tactic to make our point, to impress others, or to stimulate overreaction on their part. Exaggeration can easily extend into extreme expression and demagoguery. It is in the political arena and in connection with other efforts to satisfy or to convert that exaggeration is most likely to occur.

Labels, glittering generalities, exaggeration, and other forms of indefinite, excessive, or misleading statements are emotional expressions that make rational analysis much more difficult than would be the case if they could be avoided. They create attitudes and convictions based on incomplete or inaccurate information or misstatement of the situation that often supports what people would like to believe rather than what is accurate or true. This makes correction doubly difficult. Not only must what has been set in the mind be changed, but the correct information is usually less emotionally satisfying and may require recognizing a disturbing reality. Deliberately deceptive expression applied repeatedly and on a large scale is the governmental strategy and tactic in autocracies, rarely justified in democratic societies even in emergency situations. Where misinformation, overgeneralization, and exaggeration are most harmful is at the highest legislative and executive levels of government, where they are a way of political life for elected and appointed officials who favor expressions that can be interpreted in whatever manner is most favorable to their self-interest at the moment. If humans employ artifices to the extent that they are no longer willing or able to face reality, they will not survive.

SEPARATISM AND THE PUBLIC INTEREST

Our nation is divided into fifty states, each with its history and distinct identity, independent powers granted by the Constitution, and particular cultural and socioeconomic characteristics. Our legislators in Washington represent states and districts. They do not represent or bear immediate political allegiance to the nation as a whole. There are no U.S. legislators at large. Especially in recent years, elected representatives depend for their campaign funds on the monetary support of special interests, each concerned exclusively or primarily with its own affairs; paid lobbyists abound. Most members of the public focus first on their local and state governments, except when federal actions affect their pocketbooks or personal affairs. As noted previously, individual liberties and rights have been emphasized in the United States since its beginning. These separatist and individualistic features of our historical past and present functioning discourage a sense of individual responsibility for society as a whole. There is an absence of concern for the societal or public interest to balance our present preoccupation with our personal rights, an awareness that our separate destinies depend on the social entity of which we are only a small part. Our social concern focuses first on our family, our public interest on our home community, next on the state, nation, or other larger society of which we are part, and finally on our species spread around the world—our ultimate societal association.

> In earlier days, the individualism in America was one that also honored community values. Today we have an ideology of individualism that simply encourages people to maximize personal advantage. This leads to consumer politics in which "what's in it for me?" is all that matters, while considerations of the common good are increasingly irrelevant.[27]

"Public interest" cannot be defined exactly, although there are continuing attempts to do so. The term in generally descriptive rather than specific and certain. However, it can be explained sufficiently by example for people to intuitively and intellectually accept the concept as an essential consideration in society and an essential element in planning. It includes those activities of a society that are crucial to its successful functioning and its survival: such as a system establishing the rights of individuals and the rights or interests of the society as a collective entity; means of maintaining sufficient public order and protection of persons and property to prevent inadvertent dissolution of the society; defense against external attack; prevention of unhealthy conditions that could decimate the population; an educational system. These general provisions are subject to wide differences of opinion as to what extent and how each is attained. Their fulfillment will be different in different countries, societies, places, and times, but they represent achievements essential for the effective functioning and survival of state and local as well as national governments.

> The essence of the savings-and-loan scandal is not fraud or corruption, or even influence-buying; it is that elected officials were willing to stand by and allow large-scale swindling of their constituents. Though many people saw the debacle approaching, no one in a position of power seems to have had any interest in preventing it. . . . The public officials we elect have become—in large part because of the way we elect them—utterly incapable of defending the public interest, or even recognizing what the public interest is.[28]

Overall societal planning in the United States is now the consequence of the separate planning implicit in the multitude of different activities of governments, private enterprises, and individuals. In time, for reasons discussed throughout this book, national planning will be institutionalized in some form and made more explicit. It must continually relate separate activities and separate planning to each other and to national concerns, and identify those elements of the public interest that should receive direct governmental attention. Public interests are also a concern of private and personal enterprises. While they are not part of the general purpose or specific objective of the enterprise, they are an important or essential consideration to the extent they affect customer response, regulatory approval, efficient operations, or the use of the private activity or project.

REFERENCES

1. Foltz, Kim, "Insurance Is Sold with Wit in New Spots for Prudential," *New York Times*, 5 October 1990, p. Z C5.
2. Uchitelle, Louis, "A Lot of Spending in a Weak Period," *New York Times*, 8 October 1990, p. C2 Z.
3. Horgan, John, "Indecent Burial, Obstacles to the Disposal of Nuclear Waste Proliferate," *Scientific American*. February 1990, p. 24D.
4. "U.S. Is Faulted for Role in Water Quality," *New York Times*, 8 October 1990, p. Z A7.
5. R. P., "Face to Face with EMFs," *Science*, 21 September 1990, p. 1379.
6. Malcolm, Andrew H., "Going Beyond Jails in Drives to Make U.S. a Safer Place," *New York Times*, 10 October 1990, p. Z A9.
7. Zucherman, Mortimer B., "The Bad Guys of the S&L Fiasco," *U.S. News & Report*, 18 June 1990, p. 92.
8. Malcolm, Andrew H., "Going Beyond Jails . . . ," p. Z A9.
9. Salamon, Lester M., "The Rise of Third-Party Government: Implications for Public Management," in Donald F. Kettl, Editor, *Third-Party Government and the Public Manager: The Changing Forms of Government Action*, Summary of Proceedings and Commentary on the 1986 Spring Meeting, National Academy of Public Administration, Washington, D.C., July 1987, p. 12.
10. Ibid.
11. Cox, Wendell, "Road to Better Mass Transit Isn't Taxing," *Wall Street Journal*, 7 March 1990, p. A18.
12. Buckley, William F., Jr., *Reflections on What We Owe Our Country* (New York: Random House, 1990); quoted in Christopher Lehmann-Haupt, "How Youth Could Pay a Debt to Civilization," *New York Times*, 15 October 1990, p. B2 Z.
13. Ehlich, Thomas, "Legal Pollution," *New York Times Magazine*, 8 February 1976, p. 17.
14. Ibid.
15. "U.S. Is Faulted for Role in Water Quality," *Wall Street Journal*, 8 October 1990, p. Z A7.
16. Christian, Shirley, "Billions Flowing to Dam (and Lots Down Drain?), *New York Times*, 4 May 1990, p. A4 Z.
17. *Wall Street Journal*, 1 March 90, p. 1.
18. Hayes, Thomas C., "Former Saving Executive Sentenced to 30 Years in Jail," *New York Times*, 6 April 1990, p. C1 Z.
19. Hudson, Richard L., "Cost of Chernobyl Disaster Soars in Study," *Wall Street Journal*, 29 March 1990, p. A10.

20. MacNeil-Lehrer News Report, Public Broadcasting System (Television Channel 28, Los Angeles, California), 3 July 1990.
21. Browne, Malcolm W., "Big Science, Is It Worth the Price?," *New York Times*, 29 May 1990, p. B5.
22. Sanger, David E., "New Rift in U.S.-Japan Jet Project," *New York Times*, 20 November 1990, p. Z C1.
23. Chazanov, Mathis, "Civic Center: In 1982, the estimated cost of the project was $30 million. Now the City Council is looking at $120 million by the time the job ends," *Los Angeles Times*, 15 April 1990, p. J1.
24. Toner, Robin, " 'Wars' Wound Candidates and the Process," *New York Times*, 19 March 1990, p. A1 Z.
25. Burrough, Bryan, "The Vendetta, How American Express Orchestrated a Smear of Rival Edmond Safra," *Wall Street Journal*, 24 September 1990, p. 1.
26. Lee, Alfred McClung, and Elizabeth Briant Lee, *The Fine Art of Propaganda: A Study of Father Coughlin's Speeches* (New York: Harcourt, Brace, 1939), p. 47.
27. Bellah, Robert N., quoted in Daniel Goleman, "The Group and the Self: New Focus on a Cultural Rift," *New York Times*, 25 December 1990, p. Z 15.
28. "Notes and Comment," *New Yorker*, 24 September 1990, p. 34.

4

THE MASS MEDIA AND PLANNING

Above all, a presidential campaign is an exercise in image making, in symbolic politics and the politics of personality, whereas governing is the business of decision making, the work of substance and programs, and the politics of coalition building. The campaign rewards debating skills and theatrical talents: the dashing telegenic presence, the visual media event, the memorable one-liner for TV. But governing demands people skills: the less flashy crafts of persuasion, judgment, management, and negotiation. Campaign success often turns on exploiting temporary advantage; governing success needs patient year-in, year-out consistency and pursuit of policies.

Hedrick Smith
The Power Game, 1988

What we call the mass media of communication are recent arrivals on the human scene. Widespread newspaper circulation and use of the telephone have come about during the past 100 years. The first radio broadcast was less than 75 years ago, with television following some 25 years later. In a single human lifetime new instruments and systems of communication have been invented and developed that are affecting society almost as profoundly as the discovery of man-made fire a million or more years ago. This has occurred in an infinitesimal fraction of the time it took for the full consequences of man's being able to produce fire to develop.

PRESENT SITUATION

Today, in the United States, 93 percent of households have a telephone, 99 percent an average of five radios, over 98 percent an average of two television sets. More than 53 million American households have cable television, and almost three-quarters have video cassette recording (VCR) equipment. One-quarter of all television viewing involves cable-only channels. Newspaper circulation is some 63 million, with a readership of perhaps 126 million—one-half the population of the nation—if two people read part of the newspaper. Television is viewed by almost as many people as listen regularly to radio broadcasts and read a daily newspaper. *TV Times* has the largest circulation of any American magazine. The nation is becoming an organism interconnected by vast systems of communication that are part of the dwelling unit, installed in commercial and private vehicles, on board boats and ships, in aircraft for both crew and passengers, and carried on the person. Communication equipment is becoming smaller and smaller: walkie-talkies, wristwatch radios, computer-connected wristwatches, telephones for the suit pocket and the private car, miniature paging devices, tiny television sets, and miniature full-function computers. Such devices are being carried by more and more people, linking them together in time and space by direct, continued, and instant contact. Law enforcement officers, firefighters, news reporters, workmen on construction projects, operating and maintenance personnel report regularly to supervisors and communicate with each other as they work.

Developing countries have yet to match the breadth and intensity of intercommunication in technologically developed nations, but it is only a matter of time until income levels or government subsidy make possible a radio, telephone, or television in almost all homes in the world. "When they get extra money in the *colonia* [shanty town], the first thing they usually want to buy is a radio, then a television."[1] Mass communication, once limited to relatively few nations, has been extended by orbiting satellites receiving and transmitting electromagnetic signals to any place on earth. International long distance telephone service from the United States reaches 250 countries. A network of governmental, commercial, and private radio transmitters and receivers extends around the globe, providing scheduled programs, communication in emergencies, and informal contact among hundreds of thousands of "ham" operators. Television is now viewed by vast global audiences at the same time or separately as broadcast later. An event of universal significance or widespread human interest is broadcast immediately to all parts of the world by one or more of the electronic media. Newspapers publish special editions for distribution in regions far away from the country where their headquarters are located. Computer-generated mass mailings have increased in size, number, and international coverage. Economic markets and financial institutions around the world are linked by a global system permitting immediate transactions and providing up-to-the-minute information, soon to be operating twenty-four hours a day.

The United States has the largest number of producers of mass information: some 9,000 commercial radio stations, almost 1,400 television stations, and hundreds of newspapers. Each year some 60 billion advertising circulars are inserted in newspapers. Mass mailings to thousands or millions of people are made by any individual or organization that wishes to do so and can afford the cost. The mass media, including the telephone to a lesser extent, provide the population with most of its current information, entertainment, and recreational diversion within the household. They are also the main means of education acquired outside the school and university. Of these, television has the greatest impact. It reaches the largest percentage of people; on the average night the three major networks are viewed in some 30 million households. It is visual, the most acute form of human perception. It depicts movement, which adds to its appeal. Television is the supreme realization of the Chinese proverb that "a picture is worth a thousand words." It can be used effectively for the largest number of communicative purposes. It is not necessary to be able to read or write to absorb most of what it imparts.

Because of the significance of communication as the mechanism of interaction among members of a society, the aggregate consequences of the above developments in the mass media are greater than appears from their separate consideration. In one of its various forms, communication is the most essential element in the evolution, survival, and advancement of animal species. Chemical communication between environmental change and corresponding biological adjustment is of the essence in evolutionary development. Without sophisticated language and mass means of communication, the human species could not interact and exist societally as it does today, could not accumulate knowledge and record experience consciously, produce remarkable physical accomplishments of every size and description, and increasingly to take independent action disassociated from the gradual pace of evolution.

Of the various means of communication, television has become in the United States the most important transmitter of information in the different ways it can be conveyed by this medium.

According to the survey, most Americans get the bulk of their news from television.[2]

Studies show that more than 60 percent of voters rely on television and newspapers for their information.[3]

The majority—three-quarters—of viewers say that the first source they turn to when a major news event has occurred is television.[4]

With the average family viewing television over seven hours a day, most people's entertainment is provided by this mass medium. More sports are viewed than could possibly be seen in person. Certain broadcast stations concentrate on particular offerings: including news, sports, movies, music, family interests, religion, public affairs, adult entertainment. A number of stations now broadcast exclusively in a foreign language. Over one-half of households with television sets can choose among the programs offered on cable television.

At the present time, the extent of mass communication in the United States is found in few other countries. In some nations, however, newspaper readership or radio reception reach a larger proportion of the population than in the United States. As average income levels permit or government subsidies promote, households in most parts of the world will be connected with one or more of the electronic mass media. "[In 1990] Poland has only 3.8 telephones for every 100 people but aimed to increase that figure to 30 within 10 years with an investment of about $15 billion. . . . About 7,000 Polish villagers have no telephone, but . . . the government aims to insure that every village has at least one within two years."[5] There will continue to be great differences in the communication systems of different nations for some time to come. But unless some catastrophe occurs, what has developed and is likely to occur in the future with regard to communication in the United States will occur in time throughout the rest of the world.

FOURTH ELEMENT OF GOVERNMENT

The existing situation and anticipated developments in mass communications are vital to planning because they are the main means of covering current events, informing people concerning ongoing institutional activities and issues of their society, and presenting substantive material from the societal accumulation of basic knowledge. The mass media determine whether people are aware of or are concerned about many situations and events that shape public attitudes and reactions, within a framework of individual values initiated within the family and formed by education and experience. In democratic societies, public awareness and concern establish or constrain the agenda of governmental action. As noted earlier in this chapter, communications affect all segments of society and, as noted later, they are an important element of the economy. They are therefore part and parcel of the societal reality that is both the cause and content of all planning. The treatment of planning by the mass media determines in large part whether and how the governmental planning process in general and proposed plans in particular are formulated, undertaken, and realized.

In the United States the mass media exert such directive influence on people's lives and attitudes that they constitute in fact an element of government. The importance of newspapers in providing information and formulating opinion was recognized years ago when they were labelled "the fourth estate": implying a place alongside the legislative, executive, and judicial branches of American government. Today, more than ever before, the attitudes and political reactions of the public result from television, newspaper, and radio communication. And the exposure of the public to this communication influences its content in a reciprocal relationship that reinforces the interdependence. This is apparent in the behavior of elected officials at all levels of government whose actions and deportment are increasingly related to television exposure in the halls of government, during election campaigns, and whenever and wherever they may be televised.

> Legislators generally use television to get elected and re-elected and tend to pay attention to their local broadcasters and the three national networks because they can reach such enormous numbers of people.[6]

> It is not unusual, said the [U.S.] Senate majority leader, . . . to hear Senators discussing what kind of campaign commercial could be made from a particular vote as they stand in the well of the Senate and prepare to cast their yeas and nays.[7]

The image legislators project and the viewer response they elicit from television appearances, newspaper reports, and radio broadcasts are crucial to their election, reelection, and successful performance in office. Government can no longer be conducted without the compliance or support of the mass media of communication—not on every issue to be sure, but in general, on critical issues, and on most specific governmental initiatives and operations.

> Television has transformed the presidential office and also the governmental process. This is dangerous and potentially disastrous. Congress may be fractionated; it may speak in a cacophonous babble of 535 separate constituencies, but at least its structure is built around the serious consideration of questions of public policy. Not so television. . . . What makes good television often makes bad policy. Because of the pervasive impact of television, the actions of Presidents are directed increasingly toward the omnipresent cameras, and confined within the distorting prism of television news. Public debate is conducted increasingly in slogans and one-liners. . . . Television is a fact of life, and the President . . . will have to use television effectively in order to govern effectively. The challenge will be to find a way to use it that enlightens rather than obfuscates.[8]

The evolution of the mass media into an element of government was extended into international affairs during the ominous confrontation in the Persian Gulf in late 1990 and early 1991. The political, economic, and military moves and countermoves of the two primary antagonists and the other nations involved were developed and pursued on television around the world. In the United States this was a mixture of news, official statements, personal views, interviews, special reports, speculation, and rumor. In Iraq, as a completely controlled element of government, television served the various supportive purposes dictatorial authority decreed. An international governmental chess match was conducted on television by the political and military grandmasters concerned to bolster national and international images and multinational alliances and to weaken the political and strategic position of the adversary. It was hoped that this televised contest of national purposes would somehow resolve basic political, military, economic, moral, and religious differences without recourse to war.

By no means is television's role solely that of reporting events to several billion people by the broadcasting stations of most nations. It takes an active part in shaping public attitudes and preferences, affecting a wide range of individual and collective actions by its selection from the enormous number of current events what to present in the limited broadcast time available. Also by its manner of reporting and presentation, "indepth analysis" of developments, its choice and conduct of interviews, and by subtle editorializing. Messages are transmitted, suggestions made, and prospective "negotiations" actually conducted by leading governmental officials and prominent politicians on various television programs. Over time, such efforts and occurrences have a cumulative reality of their own. For example, by repeated reference to hostages and the way in which interviews with them and their relatives are treated, television can exert enormous influence on public attitudes, which in turn affect the conduct of confrontations involving hostages.

> However one weighs the televised give-and-take over the Administration's efforts to rally the nation for war, it confirms the difficulty of expounding policy calculations through a medium that immediately translates them into human costs. . . . To judge by the nightly reports from the Middle East, the nation's mind is less on rebuking Mr. Hussein than on safeguarding the vulnerable young Americans who from the beginning have been the focus of the television drama.[9]

The crucial role of television in reporting, initiating, and transmitting information of many kinds in modern nations is equal to the respective roles of the primary units of traditional government. In the United States, the mass media have become the "fourth power" of governance, as significant in the conduct of the nation as the legislative, executive, and judicial branches of government.

ECONOMIC ASPECTS

Besides their role in governing, the mass media constitute a significant segment of the national economy and business activity in the United States. They account for billions of dollars of capital investment in properties and equipment, large ongoing operational expenditures, and hundreds of thousands of people directly employed or indirectly dependent on the television, radio, telephone, and newspaper systems. Of these, television is the most important in terms of revenues and profits as well as the other socioeconomic impacts discussed in this chapter. The revenues of the ten major TV broadcasting companies in 1984 were $15.7 billion, yielding over $1 billion in profits: more than 6.6 percent as a share of revenues.[10] One year earlier in 1983, "the average pretax profit from VHF television in the top ten markets was about 40 percent of gross revenues."[11] "In just three years, 'The Cosby Show' has generated almost $600 million in profits from syndication to television stations."[12] "[The] value of TV stations that were sold rose from 121 million dollars in 1976 to 2.8 billion in 1984. . . . Wall Street has discovered that ownership of TV stations is tantamount to running a money machine that churns out profits in good times and bad."[13]

Television is the main medium of communication for advertising and therefore the principal recipient of advertising revenues. It influences the buying preferences, habits, and related attitudes of many million American households and supports hundreds of thousands of people producing products and services that are employed in television. The thirty-five leading advertisers in the United States spend over $7 billion of the $12 billion marketplace for television advertising. So valuable is this exposure for some companies that a thirty-second commercial on one of the three major networks costs about $350,000 in 1990 and $800,000 during the 1991 football Super Bowl broadcast. Successful performers accumulate great wealth from fees or a percentage of profits, and often as much or more from their endorsement of products.

It is clear that the ownership of TV stations is among the most lucrative investments. Television broadcasting and many associated business activities are profitable. Some cable television is struggling competitively among so many channels, but this part of the television business will remain generally profitable since almost three-quarters of households having regular TV also have cable, and most people want the diversity of programmatic choice provided by this combination. The radio, telephone, and newspaper media are also profitable, although less so than television and of course every undertaking does not succeed. The manufacturers and service organizations associated with the communication systems extend in breadth and depth throughout the U.S. economy. And as "smokestack" industries and other manufacturing are lost to foreign competition and become a smaller part of the economy, communications and other service activities become correspondingly more important.

THE IMPACT OF TELEVISION

Because it is the most expressive of the mass media, television is unique in the powers of its visual and auditory impact. When this impact is repetitive, it can create a strong and distinctive image of a person, a conceptual conviction, emotional reaction, or analytical conclusion in the minds of viewers. This effect may be the indirect consequence of any one of many presentations on TV, or the result of a direct effort "to gain friends and influence people." There are different degrees and types of identification, familiarity, or acceptance that can be established in the minds of multiple viewers.

> Broadcasting, unlike print, is not a perceived medium but a received medium. Because people must be taught to read, they learn to consciously analyze the written word. But they interpret sounds and visual images naturally and instantaneously, beginning at birth, making it easier for a communicator to affect the public with sights and sounds that evoke people's existing subconscious beliefs and desires.[14]

The most crucial impact of television is on children. They represent the future of every nation and the prospects of the next generation of the human species on earth. In the United States, young children watch television an average of four hours a day, at the early ages when they are most susceptible to the shaping forces of what is portrayed on the screen. For some, what they see on television may have more of an impact on their thoughts and attitudes than the influence of their parents, especially in the growing number of households with a single parent able to devote less time to the children. For all of them, it is the time of life when TV programs are most determinative: individually disturbing and socially disruptive, or individually and collectively constructive in their effects. "Over the years, study after study has pointed out the obvious: that children's television is a powerful educational tool, influencing the way children think and act, even what they wear and say."[15]

Adults also are influenced by what they view on television. Their feelings, emotional reactions, and thoughts concerning many matters are shaped by the selection and presentation of subjects on the TV screen. Cultural and moral values are affected by what is portrayed directly or indirectly as prevailing or proper. Desirable and permissible behavior is explicitly indicated or implicitly suggested by the thoughts expressed and the actions taken by peers or role models on television. Personal desires, tastes, consumer choice, and other preferences are affected by carefully crafted commercials. And political solicitation on TV in one form or another would not be as prevalent were its impact not known to be worth the manipulative effort to obtain free exposure or the direct cost of buying it.

Members of Congress, the President, and almost all other elected officials know that for most of them TV exposure is essential not only for election and reelection, but also to impress their constituents of their effectiveness in office. Actors and entertainers can become such popular and familiar figures that they exert a strong cultural influence particularly on the young. By repeated association with news broadcasts, program announcers can acquire a stature that is well above their actual role and the competence required to read programmatic content prepared by others. The Chrysler Corporation projected the personality and created a widely recognized image of its chairman to promote car sales by repeated appearances on television. The chief executive officer of Exxon chose television to express the company's concern and explain its actions with respect to the Valdez Bay oil spill in Alaska. The potential impact of a single appearance on television was demonstrated some years ago when an official of the company involved in an oil spill off the coast of Santa Barbara, California, belittled the environmental effects of the spill and spoke disparingly of the damage done to "a few birds." His remark triggered widespread critical reaction and was adopted as a "battle cry" by those opposing further offshore oil development at the time, and subsequently by other groups wishing to illustrate insensitive disregard of the environment. Remarks by the commentator on the television program "60 Minutes," considered prejudicial by some viewers, brought immediate and strong reaction and subsequent counterreaction. Because it reaches so many people simultaneously, television is an extremely sensitive as well as powerful medium of communication.

The power of the mass media to elicit response and engender action is demonstrated by the following remarkable accomplishment employing radio, mail, and telephone.

Mr. Dobson gets his followers' religious, political and cultural loyalty by responding to their anxieties and offering advice. For him, the machine is the radio—his programs are heard on 1,450 stations in the United States and overseas—and a staff of 700 people who answer the phones and deluge of mail seeking advice. . . . The organization he heads has an annual budget of $60 million. . . . Listeners send him 200,000 letters a month, and make more than 1,200 telephone calls daily to his organization's toll-free phone number. Focus on the Family ships out 52 million pieces of literature and more than a million cassettes a year. The organization's two main-frame computers contain information on two million correspondents.

Today, of the 10,000 letters a month that require special treatment, 1,000 are emergency cases. . . . Nineteen California licensed family counselors try to phone these people immediately. They are equipped with computerized lists of therapists and other sources of assistance throughout the nation. Mail that is special but less urgent goes to 60 staff members familiar with more than 1,000 prototype letters approved by Mr. Dobson.

Besides the half-hour weekly program featuring Mr. Dobson, Focus on the Family produces a daily 15-minute family news analysis, a weekly one-hour program, a radio drama series for children, and a brief daily program in Spanish.

Focus on the Family publishes six magazines for different age groups. A monthly political publication tells 267,000 subscribers what they can do to combat gay rights, abortion, and sexually suggestive advertising.[16]

More than radio, the impact of television extends far and wide with global consequences much greater than most people realize. Many Americans wonder why we are regarded abroad very differently than we view ourselves. We are surprised and hurt when we are called "ugly Americans." Part of this negative reaction is a consequence of our international presence and our far-flung activities. And part is the result of the image we create of ourselves in the movies and television programs we export for viewing in foreign lands. Many people abroad do not view these productions as entertainment or fiction, but believe we are and behave as portrayed on the screen and cathode-ray tube. And to an extent this is so, since every product of a society reflects its true nature in some way. When foreign audiences see violence, cruelty, crass materialism, and conspicuous consumption in the movies and television programs we elect to distribute around the world, they assume that this is our nature and this is how we behave. It is impossible to know for sure how other nations' conception of us affect the ways we interact with them. But when direct and indirect interrelationships are numerous, how nations view each other is certain to be significant in the aggregate if not in every instance.

CHARACTERISTICS AND TRENDS

There are general characteristics and trends in television as it functions today. First and foremost, it is fiercely competitive. Beginning at its source, organizations and individuals compete to own or control TV stations, to accumulate a particular group of stations, and to retain their Federal Communication Commission (FCC) licenses when they must be renewed. Stations compete among themselves to attract more viewers, obtain higher evaluative ratings, and improve their relative position, thereby enabling them to increase their advertising rates, revenues, and profits. Performers on TV compete directly or through their agents to first appear on television and then to increase the number of their appearances and to receive higher fees or salaries. Announcers vie with each other to enhance their recognition and favorable response by viewers, justifying higher pay. Writers, editors, programmers, and operating technicians and specialists of many kinds, who are never seen on the screen, compete to retain and upgrade their jobs and earn more money. To increase their own remuneration, agents battle to increase the TV exposure of their clients so that they can command higher fees for appearances, a larger percentage of residual profits, and attract more endorsements. Those owning movie rights promote their films for TV showing, and producers of proposed TV shows prepare costly "pilots" as examples, competing for the finite TV time available. Advertisers, organizations, groups, and individuals seek television exposure to promote their special interests, needs, or predilections of many kinds.

There is another dimension to this competition: the need or desire to make the most of the time attained by increasing its impact. Broadcasting stations may do this by focusing on a particular category of potential viewers, or by changes in the kind or specific content of the programs they present. Performers seek to improve the artistic quality of their performance, or more often adorn themselves to attract attention and overact with expressive exaggerations having little or nothing to do with artistry. Announcers seek to augment their reading of prepared material by including as much supplementary commentary of their own as permitted, or by as much dramatic enhancement of their presentation as allowed. Moments of silence are anathema. Writers and producers incorporate in their scripts and pilot previews whatever may entice and hold their audience. Camera crews look for new, different, or more dramatic "shots." Events are made exciting whether they are or not. The aggregate result of this continuous effort at image enhancement and greater impact on the TV audience is a built-in tendency—or a requirement in order to retain a competitive rating—to escalate the intensity or other appeal of the visual presentation and substantive content of the program. Usually this means increasing the "entertainment" or emotional appeal of the program.

The first of these is evidenced in the treatment of sports on television. What were once "games" are treated and referred to as "shows," with a larger and larger portion of the television time spent on commentary, subtitle statistics, reports on other games in progress, game-side interviews, superimposed graphics, related observations, and other items extraneous to the game itself but enhancing the role of two or more announcer-commentators and several assistants on the field, and technicians behind the scene producing the special effects on the screen. Entertainment elaborations add substantially to the cost of televising sports. " 'I'll be honest with you,' said the senior member of the ABC announcing crew. 'Show business is a big part of our business [of televising professional football games].' "[17] The emotional impact of programs that are purely entertainment may be magnified by overdramatic emphasis, increased depiction of violence, cruelty, erotic titillation, explicit sex, and catering to other human instincts and activities that civilization seeks to sublimate.

A striking example of the attraction of distorted entertainment is the continued presentation of "wrestling matches" on TV in the United States. Years ago, these ceased to be genuine matches and became entertainment shows. Men and women wrestlers affect all sorts of weird hairdress, facial adornment, and costumes, performing in pairs, foursomes, or larger teams. They appear in close-up on television before and during performances to pretend animosity by extreme declarations of superiority and hostility. Their actions in the ring have nothing to do with real wrestling, established as a sport by the Ancient Greeks in the earliest Olympic games. Their "wrestling" is carefully choreographed to appear violent and hurtful, practiced at length in gymnasia to prevent real hurt or injury. Aggressive, violent, and "illegal" actions in the ring are encouraged to stimulate live audience and TV viewer reaction. Some time ago, to obtain some operational or business advantage, the producers of TV wrestling shows petitioned that their performances be officially classified as "entertainment" rather than "sport." Real wrestling matches rarely appear on television as part of the coverage of the Olympic games or an international sports tournament. Although the complete artificiality of televised wrestling matches is known to almost all their viewers, they are sufficiently appealing as aggressive encounters to attract an audience large enough to support the cost of televised coverage. For the live audience reacting actively, the simulated hostility and violence in the wrestling ring may release some of the innate aggressiveness latent in all of us. For those sitting passively in front of their television set, it does not serve the same purpose.

The constant efforts of TV stations to capture and retain larger and larger audiences constitute a form of induced entrapment. Some observers maintain that this enticement produces viewer addiction. Whether this is the case remains to be substantiated. "The proposition that television can be addictive is proving to be more than a glib metaphor. The most intensive scientific studies of people's viewing habits are finding that for the most frequent viewers, watching television has many of the marks of a dependency like alcoholism or other addictions."[18]

GOVERNMENTAL RESPONSIBILITIES

The U.S. Federal Communications Commission is entrusted with licensing and supervising television, radio, and telephone systems so that they serve the "public convenience, interest, and necessity." This includes regulations relating to the ownership of TV stations, their operational practices, and certain limitations on language, subject matter, and programming of broadcasts. To continue to fulfill this responsibility, the FCC must be alert to developments in the future that adversely affect the character and quality of TV programs, the impact of television on its viewers and the American public at large, and its functioning in the general public interest. If the trends referred to in the previous section continue, the FCC will have to consider what they portend. And if television is indeed the fourth power of government, as suggested earlier in this chapter, the present need to see that it functions in the public interest will become a societal necessity.

Aside from the technical aspects of broadcasting that must be resolved for the several systems to operate successfully, there are important questions relating to programming that must be answered. First and foremost is the approval of those who wish to own and operate a television or radio station, and an appraisal of their performance when licenses must be renewed. The product of the station depends in large part on the primary purpose and societal attitude of its owner. In the opinion of the chairman of the National Broadcasting Company: "To the extent television gets into the hands of people just in it for an investment, that does not auger well."[19] "When asked about owning newspapers, [Robert Maxwell] had a simple answer: 'It gives me the power to raise issues effectively. In simple terms, it is a megaphone.' "[20] The influence that can be exerted by a single radio program is illustrated by the activities of Mr. Dobson referred to in the previous section.

There probably exists today an official prohibition or some form of preventive assurance that no television or radio broadcasting station deliberately or inadvertently panic the nation or any part of it. This occurred on October 30, 1938, when:

> A wave of mass hysteria seized thousands of radio listeners throughout the nation between 8:15 and 9:30 o'clock last night when a broadcast of a dramatization of H. G. Well's fantasy, "The War of the Worlds," led thousands to believe that an interplanetary conflict had started. . . . The broadcast . . . disrupted households, interrupted religious services, created traffic jams and clogged communication systems. . . . At least a score of adults required medical treatment for shock and hysteria. . . . Throughout New York families left their home, some to flee to near-by parks.[21]

While it is unlikely that broadcasts will be permitted to cause such a situation again, the susceptibility of people to overreact collectively or panic has not disappeared.

> On 3 December [1990] in southeastern Missouri, schools will be closing, factories will be shutting down, and families will be fleeing to safer ground. Why? Because that's the day [an] iconoclast scientist . . . has predicted a killer earthquake will strike. . . . Midwesterners didn't get much help from

the media in dealing with the unsettling prediction. "A lot of news people have been very noncritical." ... The media treatment of the science often consisted of statements by scientist A in favor ... and by scientist B questioning its validity. ... But many scientists noticed journalists were relying heavily on ... one of the few credentialed scientists, if not the only one, to publicly defend [the prediction], and some observers familiar with a bit of history have serious reservation about [scientist A's] suitability as a news source.[22]

Since the mass media are the chief source of information for the American people, the reliability of this information is a crucial requirement for its widespread distribution—unless misinformation is condoned or a societal policy of deliberate deception is adopted. Years ago, the newspaper columnist and literary critic, H. L. Mencken, characterized advertising as "legalized lying." This extreme and all-encompassing statement does have limited justification.

Advertising executives are still shaking their heads in amazement at North American Volvo's blatant rigging of its "monster truck" commercial. The truth is, though, that some other auto ads aren't exactly what they seem. ... "If you look at 100% literal truth, every day the consumer is getting deceived."[23]

There's real concern that informercials are being used to push bogus products. There is more than the usual share of fraudulent advertising through these informercials.[24]

Most advertising is not false, but there is enough misrepresentation to cause concern when it is broadcast to millions of people, most of whom believe what they see and hear, unless there is specific reason not to.

Even when TV is attempting to explain a confusing event or issue, having to do this in the few minutes allocated can result in greater confusion or inadvertent misrepresentation. Techniques have been developed which allow manipulation of televised material to favor particular purposes. "Increasingly sophisticated computer graphics systems are giving editors the ability to tamper with photographs in ways that suggest alternate realities. ... This rapidly spreading technology may soon allow people to present 'records' of events that never occurred."[25] Misrepresentation on television is manifested in other ways. Laughter and applause can be prerecorded and appended to all sorts of presentations to give the false impression that a live audience has reacted enthusiastically. Or a performer's presentation may be falsified: "The band ... did not do the singing on its debut album ... which sold seven million copies. ... [The performers] became international stars lip-synching their way through television and concert appearances."[26]

What represents falsification for some people is permissible exaggeration or enthusiastic endorsement for others, depending on personal morality and background. There are "gray areas" of representation in advertising and other forms of expression that people consider truthful or dishonest depending on their own individual and cultural values. There are also subtle ways of manipulating information. "As long as each sentence is accurate when read out of context, the media can string together a series of sentences that intentionally and deliberately create a false impression."[27] In the same way, pictures of a person or situation can be selected that are unflattering or in some other way instigate a negative rather than a neutral or balanced response. At the ends of the spectrum of truthful representation are areas of unquestionable honesty and dishonesty that most people recognize as such. As the mass media of communication reach more and more people, affecting their attitudes and actions, the truthfulness and reliability of the information they disseminate is essential if the media are to function constructively in society.

While deliberate misrepresentation shading into falsification is bad enough in advertising and entertainment, it is most damaging to society in television programs that are the primary source of information determining political choice by the American people. "Equal time" cannot be provided when there are numerous candidates and many issues to be covered. In fact, the advantage accrues to the candidate or special interest that can buy or otherwise secure the most effective exposure in the mass media. Accordingly, a growing number of political programs are carefully crafted by media experts to avoid discussion of the important issues and concentrate on exaggerating or misconstruing some single or several occurrences that can be used against the opponent. "1990s politics will echo with its sound bites, the 10–15-second snippets of speech endlessly repeated in the television commercials or on news reports until they come to capsulize an issue, a politician, a mood. Sound bites have become the language of politics."[28] Questionable or dishonest tactics are inherent in the ambitions of many politicians and the complete conviction of many autocrats. Exaggeration and misrepresentation on television set examples that lower the ethical standard of individuals and society as a whole. It also makes responsible planning that much more difficult.

REFERENCES

1. White, Daniel N., "Hope Flowers in a Colonia," *Princeton Alumni Weekly*, 20 March 1991, p. 14.
2. Wriston, Walter, "The Beltway–Media Complex," *Wall Street Journal*, 29 October 1990, p. A14.
3. Garamundi, John, "California's Ballot Industry," *New York Times*, 9 May 1990, p. Z A17.

4. Brown, Merrill, *How Americans Watch TV: A Nation of Grazers* (New York: CC Publishing, 1989), p. 82.
5. "Poland Sets Phone Overhaul," *New York Times*, 12 November 1990, p. Z C3.
6. Brown, Merrill, *How Americans Watch TV*, p. 45.
7. Toner, Robin, " 'Wars' Wound Candidate and the Process," *New York Times*, 19 March 1990, p. A14 Z.
8. Nixon, Richard M., "Needed: Clarity of Purpose," *Time*, 10 November 1980; quoted in Hedrick Smith, *The Power Game: How Washington Works* (New York: Random House, 1988), p. 704.
9. Goodman, Walter, "Senate Hearings on Iraq Play as TV Drama," *New York Times*, 13 December 1990, p. B4 Z.
10. Sanoff, Alvin P., et al. "Who Will Control TV?," *U.S. News & World Report*, 13 May 1985, p. 60.
11. Brown, Merrill, *How Americans Watch TV*, p. 49.
12. *New York Times*, 9 April 1990, p. C8 Z.
    13. Sanoff, Alvin P., et al., "Who Will Control TV?," p. 60.
14. Rothenberg, Randall, "A Legend Turns to Selling Change to Companies," *New York Times*, 14 January 1991, p. C8 Z.
15. O'Conner, John J., "Cartoons Teach Children But Is the Lesson Good?," *New York Times*, 20 February 1990, p. Z B1.
16. Steinfels, Peter, "Why Psychologist Without a Pulpit Is Called Religious Right's New Star," *New York Times*, 5 June 1990, p. A10 Z.
17. Eskenazi, Gerald, "TV Network Stresses the 10 in 10–1," *New York Times*, 28 November 1990, p. B10 Z.
18. Goleman, Daniel, "How Viewers Grow Addicted to Watching TV," *New York Times*, 16 October 1990, p. Z B1.
19. Sanoff, Alvin P., et al., "Who Will Control TV?," p. 60.
20. Grauman, Brigid, "D-Day for Robert Maxwell," *Avenue*, May 1990, p. 68.
21. *New York Times*, 31 October 1938, p. 1.
22. Kerr, Richard A., "Earthquake—or Earthquack?," *Science*, 26 October 1990, p. 511.
23. Miller, Krystal, "Car Marketers Test Gray Area of Truth in Advertising," *Wall Street Journal*, 19 November 1990, p. B1.
24. Winston, Joel (Assistant Director, Division of Advertising Practices, U.S. Federal Communications Commission), *Wall Street Journal*, 19 June 1990, p. B1.
25. *Los Angeles Times*, Book Review (Fred Ritchlin, *In Our Image: The Coming Revolution in Photography*, New York: Aperture, 1990), 1 July 1990, p. 10.
26. Associated Press, "Producer Says Milli Vanilli Didn't Sing Its Pop Hits," *New York Times*, 16 November 1990, p. Z B5.
27. Marcus, Amy Dockser, " 'False Impressions' Can Spur Libel Suits, Even if News Media Get the Facts Right," *Wall Street Journal*, 15 May 1990, p. B1.
28. Toner, Robin, "A Year in Sound Bites: 10 Seconds to Remember," *New York Times*, 31 December 1990, p. 29.

Part II

PLANNING FOR
THE FUTURE

5

TYPES AND APPLICATIONS OF PLANNING

All the larger evolutionary patternings seemingly favorable or unfavorable to man's conditioned reflexing are transpiring transcendentally to any man's conscious planning or contriving.

R. Buckminster Fuller
An Operating Manual for Spaceship Earth (1970)

The planning that is being conducted today is precedent to planning in the future. However much it may change or be redirected in time, what is being practiced today will continue for years to come and affect what occurs in the distant future. Planning is so widely applied that there are a host of different designations for plans which reflect the professional language or personal preference of the person conducting the planning, the field of knowledge most involved, the substantive content of the plan, its organizational affiliation, titular requirements for ready reference, or some other descriptive need. In this chapter only the basic and common categories of planning conducted in the United States today are described.

Program planning is the simplest form of planning. It exists as an intuitive directive force in the successive acts of many animals in building nests, mating, and obtaining food. It is ubiquitous in human affairs. Most personal planning requires a sequence of actions to achieve a desired result: whether it is to decide in what order shopping will be done, to arrange a trip, provide for the mortgage payments, save for a child's college education years hence, or any one of the numerous activities requiring successive steps. As the functioning of societies becomes more complex, program planning is required to engage in activities that require a lengthening list of steps, which must be taken in prescribed order. And as the societal problems noted in Part I worsen, the public will demand that political decision makers set specific objectives and indicate how they will be achieved by progressive actions.

Project planning determines the actions required to design and create a specifically defined end product within a given time and at an estimated or contracted cost. Projects involve diverse elements, some of which are indefinite and immeasurable and cannot therefore be correlated quantitatively with other elements that can be estimated and projected numerically. Projects may be physical in nature: a building, manufacturing plant, weapons system, hydroelectric dam, new town, or any one of the millions of structures that humans produce continuously. Projects are also organizational in nature, such as rearrangement of administrative units and authority, reform of elective or legislative procedures, or a new system of product marketing, distribution, and franchising. Each of these two types of projects incorporates some aspect of the other. The construction of all structures requires organization and management, but the end products of physical and administrative planning are different and each involves different knowledge and skills.

Project planning includes program planning since certain components must be completed one after another. An example familiar to most people is constructing a building. The foundations are completed first, framing next, followed by above-ground plumbing, electrical system, roofing, various installations, and finish work. Each of these components is itself effectuated by successive steps. Projects such as managerial reorganization that do not incorporate physical elements directly also are accomplished most successfully by programming a sequence of gradual changes that do not severely disrupt operations or employee morale while reorganization is under way. Project planning is more complicated than program planning because it involves a larger number and greater diversity of elements requiring a higher level of planning and management. In constructing a building these might include financing, the wishes of several controlling interests, assuring proper performance by subcontractors, changes during construction, or adjustments made necessary by unforeseen weather conditions and other developments affecting operations. Such elements cannot be programmed precisely.

As illustrated in the previous chapter, the term *comprehensive planning* signifies that the scope of consideration and analysis includes all primary elements of the organization or activity, those that determine its current condition and future prospects. Master planning is a synonymous designation used mainly in urban and regional planning, and engineers may employ the term system planning as equivalent. First and foremost, careful thought is given in comprehensive, master, or system planning to identifying the most crucial elements of the organism being planned, whatever their nature. No element is disregarded because it is intangible, indefinite, or cannot be measured mathematically. There are political, economic, and natural conditions that cannot be forecast reliably, actions by participants and antagonists that are unpredictable, and personal attitudes and behavior and group reactions that cannot be projected. Any one of these may be significant in realizing a project and must be taken into account in its planning. Comprehensive planning is practiced whenever the most significant factors are incorporated in the formulation of plans. It is not all-inclusive because it is conceptually impossible and impractical to correlate every activity, force, and event that is related directly or indirectly to what is being planned. Nor is such inclusiveness necessary since consideration of only the most significant elements is needed to simulate, plan, and manage a project or organization. Were this not the case, few human activities could be planned and conducted. Comprehensive planning often is misunderstood because many people assume that every conceivable consideration must be taken into account in the analysis; this is both practically and intellectually impossible.

Providing water for a municipality illustrates the comprehensive planning process. With respect to supply, water can come from aquifers under the city pumped from wells or from surface streams nearby. If the underground aquifers are replenished by percolation from the ground surface, intensive urban use of the land above and coverage of the ground with impermeable man-made materials reduces the replenishment and increases the runoff of precipitation. Water can be imported by conduit or other means from distant sources. If these supply agriculture as well as the municipality, increased agricultural use and farming practices can reduce the amount available for the city. Effluent from the city's sewer system can be treated and recirculated through a separate distribution system for irrigation and industrial use. It can be treated further to provide potable water reintroduced into the regular supply. Seawater can be desalinized by municipalities located near the ocean. Storage of water is required since supply and demand cannot be balanced all the time because of seasonal and other variations in demand, and variations in supply due to abnormal weather, interruption in the delivery systems, or contamination. Some reservoirs collect water from a surrounding watershed as well as store supplies from elsewhere.

Consumption varies by time of day, season, weather conditions, the needs and habits of individuals, and the equipment and appliances in the home, office, and factory that use water. Residential consumption is increased with profligate use of water for personal hygiene, food preparation, or landscaping requiring frequent and heavy watering. Total consumption increases of course when new homes, commercial establishments, and industries are built, each requiring a water connection before a certificate of occupancy is issued by the municipality. If additional water is not available or consumption is not reduced, municipal growth is curtailed.

Each of the above considerations involves a cost: direct when the money is for the construction of new facilities, indirect when by restricting growth the municipality loses tax income to a competing community with ample supplies of water. There are limitations to the costs a city can afford from taxes, fees, and other internally generated income, borrowing money, or obtaining monetary assistance from the state and federal governments. Costs vary with engineering specifications for the water system and the standards of water purity established. There are costs to be compared, such as the cost to the municipality of providing household appliances using less water free of charge, thereby reducing consumption and avoiding the costs of providing and distributing additional water. The cost of producing and distributing reclaimed water through a separate system or of desalinization must be compared with the cost of obtaining additional supplies from other sources.

There is also the problem of the "peak load." Utility systems in the United States are designed to withstand the most disruptive event that has occurred during either the past 50 or 100 years. But prolonged drought, destructive floods, operational breakdown, or some other catastrophe can occur disrupting the utility system more than any event recorded in the past. Shall the water system assure sufficient supply to meet demand under the worst conceivable conditions, or those more likely to occur? The extra capacity can be provided at great additional cost, but it will remain unused until the most improbable situation occurs. In the meantime the money spent for the super-extra capacity has not been available for other needs.

Since all of these considerations vary over time for different reasons, projections must be made every year at least ten years into the future concerning water supplies, population growth, economic and technical developments, and consumer preferences affecting the usage of water. Ten years is the approximate average lead time required today to instigate, plan, finance, and construct a physical facility of some size and complexity. Projections into the future necessarily involve probabilities—the likelihood and extent of anticipated changes. Analysis must be conducted for each consideration separately, and collectively for those that are interdependent.

Human attitudes and politics are equally or even more important elements in the analysis and planning of the municipal water supply system. If people insist on using more water, cannot be persuaded to conserve, and oppose expenditures for an increased supply of water, remedial actions must await a crisis that forces belated change in the attitudinal and political deadlock. If the people in the community will not accept the use of reclaimed water because it is psychologically too disturbing, this potential source of supply is eliminated. If expansion of the water system creates some issue inimical to the political decision makers, a prolonged stalemate can result. Comprehensive planning can develop technical plans to best meet the situation and needs all things considered, but elected representatives, the political powers that be, and the electorate must decide what to do and act to accomplish it.

As indicated in this example, comprehensive planning may invoke many considerations as analytical elements. Since most of these do not have an important effect on the operation of the project or activity being planned, comprehensive planning analysis involves the relatively few elements that adequately simulate the functioning of the organism. At some time in the future those elements that have not been taken into account are reconsidered and some of them may be reintroduced into the analysis, replacing elements that are no longer feasible or relevant. New considerations may arise.

Comprehensive planning seems so sensible one would presume it is practiced as a matter of course, but this is not the case. Those who believe the only elements to be taken into account in planning are those that can be expressed numerically and calculated mathematically regard political, behavioral, or other matters that cannot be measured precisely as analytically untreatable, even though they are vital to the operations of the organism. Others may view the functioning of the endeavor narrowly, unaware of or disregarding imprecise but significant elements. Many people do not know about the use of mathematical probability in analyzing uncertain events. For lack of knowledge or for other reasons they may consider this method unreliable or the basic concept suspect. Or there may be no one available who can make the mathematical calculations involved in statistical analysis, scientific opinion survey, engineering calculations of many kinds, or risk analysis. Those conducting the planning may be unwilling to spend the extra time and effort to deal thoughtfully and conclusively with imponderables, preferring matters that are definite and can be counted precisely.

All planning should be conducted comprehensively since no important consideration should be overlooked or ignored. But most people have not had occasion or are not motivated to consider the adequacy of planning for the task at hand. Nor are they aware of the different kinds of planning that can be applied. Attention has not been focused nor research directed toward developing methods of comprehensive planning analysis that are practicable for general use. Until more people are motivated or required to plan as effectively as possible, comprehensive planning will remain the exception rather than the rule. In governmental planning in the United States the politics, self-interest, and personal preferences of elected decision makers produce partial planning favoring the most powerful special interests. In private enterprise, all too often top management is concerned as much with personal gain as the corporate good. This conduct is most damaging at the highest levels of decision making, where the effectiveness of planning determines more than any other human factor the current condition and the future prospects of the organization or society, and in the long run whether it survives or disappears.

Planning may be short-, medium-, or long-range. The disposition of liquid monetary assets, for example, may be effected in a matter of minutes once the favorable conditions prescribed in a formal plan of action occur. *Short-range planning* is practiced by supermarkets and other stores. The sales of each item registered at check-out counters or other "points of sale" are recorded for accounting purposes and inventory management. When the inventory supply of an item is reduced to a predetermined number, reorders are automatically instigated or management is alerted to decide whether to resupply or not. Budgets constitute a planned allocation of resources for the forthcoming year, usually with at least the following year in mind since so few activities nowadays are completed in a single year. *Medium-range planning* covers the five- to ten-year period required to complete most projects. It does not extend so far into the future that the uncertainties of projection call for limitation or active opposition by those who maintain you cannot plan far ahead. *Long-range planning* can extend many years ahead. Plans for tree farming by wood products companies, for example, cover a period of some sixty years until trees are ready for harvesting, others in half this time if the trees are selected for rapid growth and use for paper pulp. Military weapons planning extends far into the future because these systems have become so technically complicated that their design, funding, development, test, production, and deployment requires longer and longer lead times. The longest-range plans involving specific steps to achieve a precise objective are probably those for a repository to isolate highly radioactive nuclear waste with a half-life of several hundred years.

Operational and *strategic planning* are different in their time spans as well as in their purposes. As the name indicates, operational plans direct the current, short-term, ongoing activities that constitute every human endeavor. Their purpose is to organize these activities so that they produce the results desired in the manner preferred. The time span is short because the current operating plan is continually modified to meet new requirements or to make improvements. For example, hundreds of modifications may be made during the time when an assembly line is producing a particular model automobile, ranging from many minor modifications in some of the thousands of parts of an automobile to a change requiring recall of the cars already manufactured. If a major revision must be made, a new plan is formulated. Families, civil governments, private enterprises, the military services, and all other human organizations follow some form of operational planning in conducting their respective activities. It may be called by another name, such as tactical planning by the military or production planning by manufacturers, or it may be unnamed but implicit in the actions taken by societal groups, families, and individuals.

Strategic planning has a much longer time span and a broader perspective than operational planning. Its purpose is to identify changes that must be made at some indefinite time in the future when the situation will be different. For example, present products will be outmoded or current sources of supply will no longer be available. It is not necessary to act immediately but the forthcoming situation must be borne in mind and plans developed in time to take care of projected needs. Some long-range strategic objectives may call for immediate action. Review of the existing situation reveals that activities have been too narrowly directed, not taking into consideration potential opportunities; or it may be that present operations when viewed as a whole should be radically reorganized over a period of time to be more efficient and to meet new conditions.

Functional planning is concerned with one element of an organization or activity. For example, there may be an explicit assignment or implicit acceptance of responsibility among individual members of a family for cooking, cleaning, maintenance, or another activity in the home. Sales, production, and finance illustrate elements in a business that are planned and managed separately in close coordination with other parts of the enterprise; each of them requires particular knowledge and experience. There are distinct differences in the operations, personnel, and planning of the police, fire, sanitation, and social service departments of local governments. And the military services are divided into functional units concerned with operations, supply, medicine, and intelligence. Plans for each of these activities are coordinated into overall operational and strategic plans.

When several functions are closely related and serve a common purpose, planning and management may be combined. Similar products or services or closely related activities, which operated as separate entities, often are combined by large corporations or holding companies into one organizational unit that manages them all together. This may permit more efficient purchase of materials, financing, or the joint use of production facilities. In a municipality, police, fire, and building and safety departments may be combined into a single unit engaged in the "protection of persons and property." Or different departments supplying electricity and gas are combined since the sources of energy will vary over time between imported natural gas, coal, oil, and for some local governments nuclear, hydroelectric, solar, or wind-generated electric energy. The proportion of total energy needs provided by each of the different sources will vary with availability, cost, conservation, environmental concerns, and other considerations. The broader scope of planning for such collections of organizational units is *subsystem planning*, often referred to in the business world as divisional or group planning.

Policies are general statements of desirable goals to be attained at some indefinite time in the future. It is not known at the time they are adopted specifically how they will be achieved. They are very different from planning objectives, which by definition incorporate the programs required for their attainment. For example, one of the goals of U.S. foreign policy is to promote democracy abroad. Affirmative action is the present policy of reducing discrimination by treating people without regard to sex, race, creed, or color. The range of possible policies or goals is as broad as the scope of human activities. In the United States today, national policies might be adopted to achieve a much improved educational system, alternate sources of energy and conservation to reduce dependence of foreign oil, a greatly increased number of affordable housing units, or a significant reduction in drug trafficking and demand. Such policies establish intentions and orient the actions of various organizations that can contribute to the realization of the goal as circumstances and available resources permit. Unlike program planning, no sequence of steps can be identified at any given time that will achieve the desired result. Steps are taken toward the goal as opportunities arise. Since the most crucial societal goals are also the most difficult to resolve, their attainment requires years of intermittent but consistent effort. A program of progress to achieve these goals cannot be formulated at the time the policy is adopted. The time required for realization is too long, the elements involved too many, and the factors that determine progress and ultimate success too diverse and indefinite. Whatever means exist or become available and can be applied are utilized. Some constructive steps are politically feasible and economically possible immediately; others occur at various times in the future. Long-range policies are not realized until some time in the distant future. Some are never realized but provide a continuation of effort that produces worthwhile results.

Policy planning sets "a course of action, guiding principle, or procedure considered to be expedient, prudent, or advantageous . . . a plan or course of action as of a government, political party, or business, designed to influence and determine decisions, actions, and other matters."[1] Policies are not limited to the societal and governmental levels where they have the most widespread effects. Any organization or individual can adopt policies defining goals and governing behavior. Policy planning and implementation are particularly difficult in democracies because as Prime Minister Winston Churchill pointed out forty years ago in his book concerning the years preceding World War II:

> The structures and habits of democratic states, unless they are welded into
> larger organisms, lack those elements of persistence and conviction which

can alone give security to humble masses; . . . even in matters of self-preservation, no policy is pursued for ten or fifteen years at a time. We shall see how the counsels of prudence and restraint may become the prime agents of mortal danger; how the middle course adopted from desires for safety and a quiet life may be found to lead direct to the bulls-eye of disaster.[2]

Although Winston Churchill's admonition referred to the failure to stop Adolf Hitler early on, his observations apply equally to peacetime policies. As noted in several connections in this book, human activities are complicated by advances in science and technology. Longer lead times are required to complete projects as they become technically more complex. Ever-longer periods are needed to attain societal goals, which are difficult to achieve because they seek to resolve basic problems and are broad in scope with widespread effects. During the period of working toward the attainment of a goal, continuous attention must be paid by those concerned to take advantage of opportunities that arise to make progress. Many people believe that scientific and technical accomplishments increase society's capability to plan and manage its affairs constructively and attain longer range goals. Whether this is the case or not, goals cannot be realized if public and political preferences and priorities change so often that policies to attain them are not adopted and pursued for a long enough time—or people presume societal problems will somehow be resolved without effective planning. In either case the society is weakened if it is unable to act consistently and progressively. If this continues long enough, the stability and future of the society are threatened.

The terms for the other main types and applications of planning are self-explanatory. *Civil governmental planning* is practiced at national, state, regional, and local levels. Planning at the national level is conducted by the departments and independent agencies of the federal government and their components. This planning is incorporated in a vast array of governmental concerns and activities, for example: monetary policy planning by the Federal Reserve Board; commercial airline routes, requirements, and regulations by the Federal Aviation Agency; military activities by the Department of Defense; agricultural programs of many kinds by the Department of Agriculture; the federal judiciary system by the Department of Justice; regulation of the mass media by the Federal Communications Commission. These few illustrations barely suggest the diversity of planned activities covering the nation as a whole conducted from Washington and from the regional and district offices of the federal departments and independent agencies. All of these organizations plan their own activities in order to function. At the present time, however, there is no integration of their separate plans and activities with reference to the total resources of the nation and its primary requirements, concerns, specific objectives, and policy goals. Congress, the president and his executive office, and the Supreme Court in its role of judicial review come closest to acting together in the collective best interest of the nation as a whole. But effective integration is impossible until there is a common reference of analytic facts and figures, a record of ongoing activities and commitments, and their projection into the future available to both the executive and legislative branches of government.

The extent of *state planning* varies greatly among the fifty states. Besides the functional planning by state departments, districts, and other agencies that they perform in fulfilling their responsibilities, some have programs coordinating state activities and reviewing the local land-use plans of counties, municipalities, and local districts. Most recently, several states have introduced a regional level of government to coordinate land-use planning by local governments within areas having common characteristics. Normally, their spatial jurisdictions coincide with county boundaries in order to avoid to the extent possible the analytical difficulty and expense of having to correlate current and historical data that refer to different areas on the ground. Some states limit their planning to the operations of the units of the state government. Most municipalities and counties have established *local planning* commissions and supporting departments to prepare and maintain land-use plans for the areas within their boundaries as recommendations for adoption and implementation by their legislative bodies. In all civil governmental planning in the United States, elected legislatures determine the type and extent of comprehensive planning that will be undertaken by each unit of government within their jurisdiction.

Planning takes place within the legal jurisdiction of civil governments, or within areas delineated by government, business, or one of the military services for a particular purpose. The geographical features of the earth, however, exist within areas of different size and spatial characteristics determined by evolutionary forces and events in the natural environment. Rarely do these natural areas or regions coincide with the jurisdictional boundaries established by man throughout history to designate political and administrative domains.

Regional planning has to do with these spaces as they occur in nature and are delineated by man for various purposes, such as gathering information, spatial designation or analysis, business administration, military operations, provision of services, emergency relief, or research. Most of them are employed for a single purpose. They may be short-lived or long-lasting. Only recently have they been incorporated as legal elements in the governments of several states in the United States.

Metropolitan regional planning relates to the contiguous urbanized areas that have been created around the world by the migration of people from rural regions to cities. They usually include many municipalities legally independent but spatially indistinguishable on the ground, with many activities and problems in common producing regionwide duplications and contradictions of effort. Metropolitan governments are proposed for these regions by public administrators, and several have been established in North America.

Although the military services are part of civil government—except in military dictatorships where they are pre-eminent—*military planning* is distinctive in several respects. The objectives adopted by civil governments change with inevitable shifts in public and political attitudes, socioeconomic conditions, and circumstances. Much of the time civil objectives are uncertain and unclear. Those of the military establishment are definite and fixed: national defense, protection of vital national interests, or action against enemy threats. While civil governments work toward some objectives continually and achieve some of them in part, military objectives for wartime contingencies are not realized until the planned military operations are undertaken at some time in the future. In peacetime, efforts are directed to the preparation of strategic and tactical war plans to meet the many situations which could arise requiring military action; the organization, training, and equipment of armed forces to meet these contingencies; the development and production of new weapons systems in a state of readiness. The best way of meeting the hypothetical situations with the funds provided during peacetime and of conducting operations in wartime are debated, but the ultimate objective remains the same. This constant purpose permits the formulation of complete and detailed plans, which are modified or abandoned if the situation postulated has changed when the time for implementation arrives.

The emphasis on planning by the military is required by both political and military leadership and accepted by the public. This is in sharp contrast with the difficulties encountered in establishing plans for civil governmental activities. The human and material resources required to plan for the military contingencies recognized by the national government are provided. They consist of elements that can be counted, destructive forces that can be measured, and probabilities that can be calculated based on experience and test results. The chain of command and control is firmly established. The peacetime functioning of operational units can be evaluated in practice exercises on the ground, at sea, and in the air. There are intangibles that are considered and reflected in war plans, such as the morale of military personnel in wartime and the supportive attitudes and actions of the families of servicemen and -women and the civilian population at home. Deliberate deception and psychological warfare may be important. Military plans as a whole are the most comprehensive, specific, quantitative, and thoroughly prepared in the United States today. The scientific and technical content is greater and more advanced than in any other form of governmental planning.

Many new technologies, products, and devices first developed for military use are passed on with or without modification for civilian use in peacetime. Planning as a staff activity supporting executive decision makers originated in the military concept of "line" and "staff" activities and organization. The distinction between "strategic" and "tactical" or operational plans relates to the need for broad-scale plans covering military activities as a whole over a longer period of time than those required for the disposition and movements of specific combat units in battle. Grouping people into sections, departments, divisions, groups, and corporations in business and into comparable units in government probably was borrowed from military organization into platoons, companies, regiments, brigades, divisions, and armies. The succession of management levels in government and business also reflects the military chain of command and control. As society and warfare have developed and changed over time, so have military procedures and the relationship between military and civilian concepts and practices.

Planning has been as essential in business since its beginning as it has been in other human endeavors. Today, business success depends on planning its research and development, financing, product selection, sales and marketing, manufacturing or provision of services, distribution, public and governmental relations, and every aspect of its activities. Planning is conducted at all levels of business organizations by managers, supervisors, and individual workers. There are more and more positions that include the word plan in their official designation. *Business planning* by top management in larger companies usually is referred to in organization charts and in general as *corporate planning*. Its extent is indicated by the existence of an International Society of Planning and Strategic Management, an Operations Research Society of America, and an Institute of Management Science with a combined membership of many thousands in the United States and abroad. In recent years business planning has expanded its spatial scope as business operations extend around the globe.

Similarly, the federal government takes into account in its planning such global considerations as the economic and monetary policies of industrial nations abroad, international trade as it affects the fiscal balance of trade, foreign investment in the United States supporting growth, or scientific and technological developments affecting American business. State and local governments also adjust their planning to the availability and cost of imported oil, needed products from abroad, foreign investment financing growth, and events elsewhere in the world influencing the state and local situation. *International planning* has occurred among nations concerning monetary policy, the transmission of acid rain between countries, and most recently coordination of military strategy, operations, and other support among the nations united in opposition to the invasion and annexation of Kuwait by Iraq. *Global planning* may be developing to reduce climatic warming, depletion of the protective ozone layer in the upper atmosphere, accidental nuclear and other pollution, and infections threatening the human species around the world.

Emergency or *contingent plans* are commonplace. For example, fire escapes and smoke alarms are part of an emergency escape plan. Back-up electric generators are installed in hospitals to provide power in operating and recovery rooms and other critical areas when local power sources fail. Emergency plans are required for immediate evacuation from around nuclear power plants. Police, fire, traffic, and sanitation departments have contingency plans that they activate when a disaster, disruptive event, or system failure requires immediate and concentrated remedial response. On a small scale, the redundancy built into many engineered systems provides for continued operation if the primary system fails, producing a minor or major emergency depending on what the system controls. On a large scale over a period of more than 100 years, the U.S. Corps of Engineers has completed a succession of emergency or contingency plans to contain the Mississippi River and prevent destructive flooding of large areas within the one-third of the continental United States that it drains. This has involved dozens of flood-control projects costing billions of dollars.

The more common forms of planning practiced today described in this chapter will continue to be applied in human affairs. Since they are the modern manifestation of the directive force originating millions of years ago that is innate in human development and behavior, they will persist as an essential aspect of people's existence. Like any other human activity, many plans are ill-conceived, unsuccessful, or never carried out, but on balance, planning has been successful enough to make possible the remarkable achievements of human beings and the progress of civilization. This has been particularly apparent during the past several hundred years. New kinds of planning will be developed and methods of analysis will be improved. Every indication points to the need and necessity of more and better planning in the years to come. Whether it will be applied beneficially by the human species remains to be seen.

REFERENCES

1. *American Heritage Dictionary*, Second College Edition (Boston: Houghton Mifflin, 1982), p. 959.
2. Churchill, Winston S., *The Second World War, The Gathering Storm* (Boston: Houghton Mifflin, 1948), pp. 17, 18.

6

ADVANCING PLANNING EDUCATION AND KNOWLEDGE

The process by which a team of planners is able to assemble and reduce to reciprocal relatedness the materials furnished by the ordinary techniques of political science, economics, sociology, anthropology, engineering, and architecture, and by which it projects a composite future, is the unique possession of this discipline.

The academic study of planning has been cast generally in terms of "city planning" or "regional planning"—the areal emphasis—and so has concentrated on improvements in the utilization of the space-volume dimension. Perhaps only by being freed from the domination of practice—or, to put it another way, by utilizing practice for illumination rather than guidance—can the theory of conjuncture and the psychology of collective thinking be advanced.

That the study of planning, then, will come to be recognized as another among the social sciences may be predicted with some confidence.

Rexford G. Tugwell
"The Study of Planning
as a Scientific Endeavor," 1948

Planning as a special subject of study and intellectual discipline has five historical roots. Public and business administration have incorporated planning as an essential component since their innovation as fields of professional practice, education, and research. Architecture and landscape architecture have included land planning as a minor concentration in their curriculum preparing students for subsequent practice. Accredited graduate programs in urban and regional planning in some sixty universities focus on land-use planning in cities, metropolitan urban areas, and regions. However, in each of these five fields, planning has been treated as a minor consideration, and none of them include one or more indispensable elements of comprehensive planning. Public and business administration treat physical-spatial planning superficially if at all. Architecture, landscape architecture, and urban and regional planning do not concern themselves directly with fiscal and budgetary matters, the politics of governing, or organizational management, which are necessary parts of comprehensive planning.

ANALYSIS

As explained and exemplified in Chapter 5, comprehensive planning takes into account the primary elements that normally constitute and determine the functioning of an activity or organization. Usually some elements, such as political and public relations or the attitudes of individuals, cannot be measured by numbers but may be crucial to success. When the primary elements are analyzed together for planning purposes, those that can be reliably quantified must be integrated with those that require evaluative judgments concerning their relative importance and their relation to other elements. This difficult integrative analysis is essential at the topmost and final level of decision making which determines more than any other managerial input the success or failure of the organization or activity. This fact alone signifies the importance of comprehensive planning as a process and intellectual discipline. It requires the highest human competence employing the best procedural means and analytical methods available. It calls for continuing research and educational programs to advance the field as a beneficial process and an area of substantive study. At present there is no such endeavor but several academic and research programs have come close enough to indicate desirable features when it is established.

Methods of analysis will be advanced continually by their field of origin and primary association. Mathematics will improve statistical analysis, the calculation of probabilities, risk analysis, artificial intelligence, game and chaos theory, and the phenomenon of self-organized criticality. How best to employ such methods in rational planning will be determined as they develop. Psychological research will enable us to better understand the behavior of individual people, groups, and large populations, particularly the forces that operate below the level of consciousness but significantly affect our conscious emotional reactions and thinking. For example, is personal judgment—the simplest and also the most universally employed analytical method—subject to biases and prejudices that we only partly recognize or may not be aware of at all? Are there ways we can identify such dynamics affecting our judgment and compensate for them, improving the objectivity and accuracy of our judgments?

Some level of prejudice is almost inevitable, even in people who feel that prejudice is wrong. . . . Psychologists are saying it may be more practical to try to suppress the expression of prejudice rather than eliminate the feeling. . . . The stubborn prejudice that some people do not shake may explain recent findings that bias acts have increased even while, on the whole, levels of bias have fallen.[1]

Because the desires of people are the purpose of plans in democratic societies and people are inevitably involved in their formulation and realization, planning benefits the more we know about how people act and react individually and in groups.

Theoretically, all fields of knowledge are involved in human activities, directly and immediately or indirectly and many steps removed. But man can cope mentally and practically with only a few of these at a time. This is why relatively few components can be consciously considered in any human action. And it is why only the primary elements of the organism are analyzed in comprehensive planning.

PROCESS

Process is important in planning. In what order are parts of plans formulated and in what sequence are they carried out, by whom in what way? The procedure can be efficient and brief, or bureaucratic and drawn out—creating problems for those who must wait for plans to be drawn or for those who await their realization. While there are basic similarities in the way all planning is conducted, there are procedural differences in how it is performed in government, business, and the military services. For example, democratic government incorporates different degrees of public exposure and the rule and procedures of law. Business planning in the United States is characterized by executive decision and specific directives, but recently some large companies have introduced participation by employee groups in planning and decision making at different levels of the organization because this has proven so successful in Japan. The Prussian army was the first to establish special staffs to assist line commanders in preparing war plans and carrying them out in combat. This organizational innovation by the army some 180 years ago was adopted by the other military services and later by government and business. Because of such transfers of knowledge and practice in the past, the process of planning merits continuing study not only to improve performance in each kind of planning but also to identify features in one application that can be adopted to advantage by another.

PRACTITIONERS

Although planning is intrinsic in human activity, it is practiced more deliberately and intensely in two applications: staff planning and planning by executives as part of their management of operations in business organizations, ranking officers exercising military command, and government officials in a position to support or require planning as a desirable or necessary activity. Different personal characteristics and qualities are needed to perform successfully in these two general categories of planning.

Staff planners assist business executives, commanding generals, and ranking government officials in fulfilling their institutional responsibilities and attaining their personal objectives. Business executives and commanding generals consider planning a primary requirement for successful performance. Planning is much less important in the minds of government officials who focus their efforts mainly on politics and reelection or reappointment. Most managers are called upon continually to take the lead in resolving critical problems and responding to emergency situations, as well as to direct the regular operations of the business organization or the military unit with which they are affiliated. Particular information and special analytical studies are needed as background for sound executive decisions and constructive actions—all the more as human affairs become more complicated. Line executives hardly have time enough to perform their managerial duties, much less prepare their own special reference materials. These are produced and maintained by planning staffs, which are becoming essential elements in the successful management of large organizations. The staffs of elected executives and legislators are often so much more knowledgeable about political issues and legislative matters than the officials they serve that lobbyists often seek to influence a member of his or her staff rather than the official.

Besides a genuine interest in and understanding of the planning process, staff planners must have analytical capability since this will be their primary responsibility. They need to be keen observers, alert and intelligent, with good judgment and a comprehensive view unimpaired by blind spots or prejudices distorting analytical conclusions. They should have a perceptive understanding of human behavior. On larger staffs there may be individuals who do not meet all of these criteria but provide a particular expertise. Staff planners must be comfortable in their role of supporting a superior who makes the executive decisions, without resenting that they can only recommend. This requires a temporary reversal of roles for line executives who are assigned to staff planning for several years to learn more about planning and how to use it themselves when they return to directing operations. Some business corporations assign young executives to the corporate planning staff as part of their experience and career advancement, and this is a regular procedure for ranking military officers.

Managing executives in business and line officers in the military services are individuals who seek or can accept responsibility. They are willing to be judged and compensated by their performance in producing profitable or otherwise successful goods and services. They are comfortable making decisions, taking action, and taking chances. They are leaders rather than followers, doers more than contemplative thinkers. They gain respect and exert authority. To plan comprehensively and successfully in industrialized societies today, they must be able to thoughtfully evaluate what is the best course of action. Precipitous reaction or intuitive "seat-of-the-pants" management will almost always produce unfortunate consequences. With analytical material prepared by their staff, they must make difficult decisions that require careful study: what risks are statistically worth taking; when machinery or equipment that is still functioning profitably should be replaced by improved models; whether or when to introduce new products or services or enter new market areas; how much money should be spent on research and development for what purposes; or what competitors are able and likely to do in the future. Such questions require background information and careful analytical thought before decisions are made and action taken.

Since line executives and officials applying comprehensive planning in their management of operations are far more numerous than staff planners, they will have the greatest influence on confirming and extending the art and science of planning. But staff planners are more likely to advance the basic theory of planning. This is because they determine specifically and conduct the process of planning, and maintain its analytical accuracy, in accordance with the desires of the operating executive to whom they report. Their time and attention are devoted to the process of planning itself, rather than its application to the organizational entity by the operating manager. They are continually involved with theoretical questions and answers.

EDUCATION

Comprehensive planning is an *analytical process* that can be applied in every area of human endeavor. It involves gathering descriptive information concerning the project or activity being planned, simulating its functioning so that the effects of suggested actions can be tested, evaluating current operations, formulating a plan of action, implementing the plan, and revising it as needed. It is a continuous process with modifications made and new plans formulated and implemented as conditions change. The body of knowledge required to perform this analytical process successfully constitutes the intellectual discipline of comprehensive planning and the subject matter of education in this field of academic concentration, human endeavor, and professional practice.

Since the range of rational planning is as broad as the scope of human affairs, all knowledge is relevant, but only a tiny fraction of this vast accumulation is needed at any one time in connection with a particular employment of the planning process. Comprehensive planning incorporates knowledge from whatever sources can provide it. Substantive material from chemistry, physics, biology, psychology, or any other body of knowledge is incorporated in planning a project or activity that involves a particular academic field. Some fields are involved in most comprehensive planning: economics, politics, law, management, engineering. Techniques developed by a number of closely related disciplines are employed almost universally in planning: statistical and risk analysis, forecasting, economic evaluation and accounting, the psychological analysis of human behavior. The range of consideration in comprehensive planning is broad, but as has been pointed out, it can be reduced to the comparatively few elements that determine the functioning of the organism, are intellectually comprehensible, and analytically manageable.

Graduate education in comprehensive planning begins with the selection of students. The contents of this book should make clear that the importance and difficulty of planning comprehensively requires superior students such as those accepted by the leading U.S. law, medical, and business graduate schools. They should come well equipped in the basic requirements of effective personal communication: verbal articulateness, literacy, and computer competence. With the sorry state of undergraduate education in the United States today, these basic capabilities cannot be taken for granted. Students should be motivated on first arrival toward planning as a field of study, a crucial process in executive management, and a field of professional practice. They should be intelligent, emotionally mature, realistic, broad-minded, oriented toward the future, interested in making improvements and effective with people.

The curriculum should include instruction covering the knowledge and specific techniques needed to perform the analytical process of comprehensive planning described at the beginning of this section on education.

Factual information is required to describe the functioning of what is being planned. The social sciences are often slow to spot and reluctant to employ new sources of information. For example, urban and regional planning and public and business administration do not introduce their students to optical, radar, and other electromagnetic remote sensing although it provides a larger quantity and greater diversity of information for planning purposes than any other source, including the U.S. census. The characteristics of information should be known to its serious users and its reliability determined before it is utilized in planning analysis.

Simulation is the heart of planning analysis. It takes different forms depending on the nature of what is being planned. Accounting spreadsheets of operational and financial data can represent business. Line drawings or computer graphics, written specifications, and physical scale models depict many buildings and structures in their finished form. Mathematical models are employed when the functioning of what is being planned can be expressed by numbers and mathematical interrelationships. Artificial intelligence surrogates human judgment in operational situations where experience has established the conditions to be expected, the considerations to be taken into account, and the proper responsive decisions. Corporate and city planning centers have been designed to facilitate and improve comprehensive planning and executive decisions in these two applications of the process by representing the functioning of the company or municipality by a combination of numerical, graphical, and pictorial displays, written material, mathematical formulations, and whatever best expresses the elements to be considered and their interactions.

Means of evaluating current operations range from their profitability in the short run or over the long term in business, the observed consequences of administrative organization or particular legislation in government, or the destructive effects of military weapons systems. As the most common means of evaluation, individual and collective judgment merits continuing study concerning its derivation, scope, and reliability and ways it can be improved, formulated as a group opinion, affected, and manipulated by the way it is elicited.

Plans are formulated in many ways: within the mind, on paper, on the computer screen, or employing physical models; by a single individual with or without consultation, a group of people, or an entire population; by a central political authority, organizational headquarters, or decentralized participation; autocratically or democratically; as an end-state condition or a continually adjusted process; as a statement of policies or a specific program of sequential actions. Each form is appropriate to a particular situation and a certain set of conditions.

Even the most dictatorial plans involve accommodation between the ideal or desirable and the attainable. The formulation and implementation of plans in real life almost always requires reconciliation of different interests and opposing opinions. The art and incipient science of negotiation and compromise is therefore an important element in comprehensive planning education. It cannot be ignored as it has been in closely related academic programs.

These are some of the factors to be considered in comprehensive planning analysis. They exemplify its educational subject matter. They also indicate the importance of the faculty having experience in some application of planning in the real world of government, business, or one of the military services. This can be acquired before or within several years after joining the faculty. Opportunities to acquire this experience by direct participation exist within the community or can be arranged to provide equivalent exposure to planning in practice. Regular contact with organizations and individuals outside the university engaged in different kinds and applications of planning should be maintained by the faculty and arranged for students. Laboratory and workshop courses can be organized around case studies of concern to sponsoring agencies that underwrite the modest expenses of such courses. Planning practitioners should be invited to present their knowledge to the graduate students in special lectures or by participating in seminars. This is important not only to prevent academic isolation, but also because the "cutting edge" of the field employing new knowledge and the most advanced technique often is found in organizations practicing planning rather than within the ivy-covered walls of academe.

Curricula should be reviewed at least every few years, or whenever a development occurs that alters or expands the intellectual content of the field. Some worthwhile improvement always can be made at the time of regular review. New knowledge may have emerged. Developments in the practice of planning may affect comprehensive planning analysis. A particular course is no longer the best use of the time available. Except for a master's thesis or the doctoral dissertation, graduate curricula are limited to a maximum number of hours of instruction for all required and elective courses. This finite time should be spent on the very best selection of subject matter.

As sensible as such review may be, it is successfully resisted by most university faculties. Professors want to do what they want to do when they want to do it. They want to teach only those courses that are most appealing to them at any given time. They resist teaching a course that provides part of the best curriculum content but is not their favorite. Each professor believes that he or she alone can decide the relevance of their courses to comprehensive planning analysis and precisely what they should cover. If there is a portion of a course that would be better taught by someone else who knows more about the topic, the instructor resists the idea of shared teaching—or "team teaching" as it is derisively called by some professors—although the rapid expansion of knowledge in recent decades demonstrates the desirability or necessity of collaboration in teaching certain subjects. Since comprehensive planning is in an early stage of consideration and development it is especially important that graduate curricula are evaluated periodically regardless of bureaucratic inertia or the reluctance of some faculty.

RESEARCH

Research is essential for the advancement of every body of knowledge and every field of activity and professional practice. It is especially crucial in comprehensive analysis because of the significance of planning in all areas of human activity. The number and scope of activities noted in this book, and the diverse sources cited as supporting references, indicate the range and potential contribution of related research. Comprehensive planning is required for successful operations by so many different organisms that many of them will conduct formal or informal research to improve managerial performance and profitable operations. Research will be a natural product of graduate programs in comprehensive planning education when they are established. In time a computer network may maintain a reference record of such research under way and completed.

Simulation

Simulation is the method of representing what is being planned by determining which of its many components closely describe its functioning, how these primary elements operate separately, and how they interact with each other. This analytical representation enables a manager or planner to ascertain the effects of various assumptions, possible developments, and proposed actions on each of the primary elements and the functioning of the project or activity as a whole. The simulation must not only accurately depict current operations, but also indicate how the organism would function in the future under different conditions and in response to different managerial decisions. As noted briefly earlier in this chapter, simulation takes many forms depending on what is being planned.

Usually, some of the descriptive elements cannot be numerated and compared mathematically. They must be represented in some other way that permits meaningful comparison with the other components of the analytical simulation. Methods of reliably projecting the elements of the simulation separately and together are part of the analytical planning process. Different ways of formulating, presenting, and displaying analytical representations affects their intelligibility and regular use by decision makers. Advancing the accuracy and effective employment of simulations is a primary objective of continuing research because representative analysis is the core of comprehensive planning.[2]

Procedure

Although there are common features in the process of formulating and implementing plans, there are differences in specific procedure, detailed treatment, or relative emphasis. The process is adjusted to the particular political, socioeconomic, environmental, and other conditions under which the planning is undertaken and carried out. The time available to formulate and effectuate a plan compresses or extends the process and alters the precise procedure. There are differences between plans depending on the organizations and institutions involved in their effectuation. For example, the extent of public participation that is required, desired, or permitted varies among societies. Research reveals ways of improving planning procedure and programming specific actions in sequence and operational detail. Research also is needed to answer the critical questions raised in previous chapters concerning how the mass media of communication relate to the success, failure, and process of comprehensive planning.

Human Behavior

People are the most important and ultimate consideration in planning. Its purpose is to attain human objectives: a specific product or outcome for a person or a number of people, designated improvement in the condition of a group of people, or advancement of human welfare in general. People instigate and conduct the planning process: formulating and implementing plans. They live with the consequences of planning, successful or failing, good or bad. Each of the many interrelationships between people and planning involves different behavioral considerations. What are essential and desirable human objectives for planning? What personal characteristics affect people's capability to formulate sound plans and to carry them out effectively with the least contention or antagonistic reaction? Are there ways of encouraging people to acknowledge unpleasant or discouraging realities, to do something about them, to act collectively, to subordinate self-interest at times in favor of the public interest, to forego some immediate benefits for longer-range results? These are some of the questions raised in Chapter 2 and 3 that indicate the importance of psychological and sociological research directed at greater understanding of human behavior in connection with planning and the society in which it takes place.

REFERENCES

1. Goleman, Daniel, "New Way to Battle Bias: Fight Acts, Not Feelings," *New York Times*, 16 July 1991, p. Z B1.
2. Branch, Melville C., *Continuous City Planning* (Chicago: American Society of Planning Officials, Planning Advisory Service, Report 290, April 1973).

7

SOCIETAL SITUATION AND THE FUTURE OF PLANNING

The fact is, most humans are not concerned with truth; they are concerned with political survival. If enough people share an illusion, they amount to an army—of votes, if not of armed personnel. Crusades occur, mass exterminations, military buildups, as do movements in arts, religion, science, philosophy—all based on the passions with which people embrace their illusions....

The cerebral cortex sits atop the limbic system and the reptilian complex, and when all is said and decided, the rational mind serves the four F's: fleeing, fighting, feeding, etc....

The ideas we learn in childhood become "imprinted" in our minds, and the normal human is not capable of and/or not interested in discarding the beliefs and values acquired in childhood. Life is too short. There is too much to lose. There is too much anxiety, too many chances to fail in starting over. Evolution has solved this dilemma with one of its most brilliant inventions. It is known as denial, the bodyguard of false illusion. *Homo sapiens* possess an absolutely fabulous ability to deny the truth....And so we come to the ultimate test of the human mind: the salvation of the environment. Can *Homo sapiens* survive the threat of itself? In light of its capacity for false illusion and its phenomenal capacity for denial can it even conceive the issues?

William Jordan
Divorce Among the Gulls,
An Uncommon Look at Human Nature (1991)

As noted in several connections in this book, planning is involved in our daily activities, and we engage in increasingly complicated processes and construct larger and larger projects requiring a high order of planning. We learn from accumulated experience how to plan more effectively.

Despite this universality, planning has not received the attention it merits as an integral element of human functioning and survival.

Civil governments, businesses, and the military services have each developed their particular means and methods of planning. While these applications differ in significant ways, the basic process is the same. The information needed to understand the functioning of the organization or activity being planned must be acquired. An analytical representation is formulated that simulates the organization or activity so that the effects of different events, actions, or decisions can be studied. From this analysis conclusions are reached concerning what is needed and what can be accomplished. A plan is prepared to achieve feasible objectives. It is carried out and the results observed to determine what modifications should be made in the continuous process of planning to improve performance. In most of its applications, the process of planning is not so clearly identified. It is disregarded or taken for granted without realizing that there is much to be learned about the successive steps in the process: the background knowledge required, different techniques of analysis, and the most effective procedural methods of implementation. As noted in the previous chapter, continuing research directed toward determining how planning is conducted most effectively will advance fundamental knowledge concerning the process and field of study and activity, make generally available the lessons learned from both successful and unsuccessful experience, and reduce needless mistakes in practice.

PLANNING EXPOSURE

The major professional practitioners of planning do not systematically communicate their experience and investigation with each other. Most businesses treat their plans as "company confidential" to avoid disclosing to competitors their current condition, their present intentions, and specific objectives. Most military plans are classified for national security reasons. Some states have enacted laws requiring legislative sessions to be conducted in public rather than behind closed doors; others conduct formal legislative business in public as a preferred policy rather than a legal requirement. Nevertheless, many governmental plans are not disclosed specifically to avoid controversy, opposition, or possible embarrassment. There is little reporting of planning practices and experience by the mass media of communication. And most of this has to do with failures, which are considered more newsworthy than successes.

The professional literature having to do with the process of planning per se rather than particular applications is minimal, partly because of restrictions on disclosure but more importantly because the significance of planning in human affairs is not yet recognized by most fields of knowledge, professions, and the public at large. Even public administration, business management, and engineering do not treat the process of planning adequately although they consider it an essential part of their field of knowledge and professional activity. Engineers rarely publish their experience and the conclusions they reach concerning the planning they perform as an element in their design and construction of a multitude of projects and operating systems around the world. Most believe the final products speak for themselves without any explanation of how they were realized. Other professions overlook or discount planning as a crucial directive process in the conduct of human affairs. However, as human activities require more and more forethought, every profession can be expected to explore to a greater extent than is the case today the role of planning in its advancement as a field of knowledge and its successful employment in practice.

People in general have little occasion to be aware of the universality and importance of planning, except when they consciously practice it themselves in their own activities, or when they, their family, or their friends are affected directly by a plan of some organization. And when the plan is no longer of concern, whatever interest in the planning process was associated with it disappears quickly. To alert the public to the extent and significance of planning requires a deliberate explanatory effort over a considerable period. The time required and the means and methods employed will differ greatly among nations, depending on the educational level and cultural characteristics of the population. In economically and technologically developed countries, the mass media can provide the immediate and continuing communication with the populace required. In other societies the message can be imparted—more slowly to be sure but in time successfully—by word of mouth exercised irregularly but persistently and by associating communication explaining planning with regular contacts between public organizations and people whenever they occur. Every government possesses the means and methods of alerting people sooner or later to the role of planning in human activities in general, and more specifically, to the part it plays in the attainment of individual and group objectives.

Motivating the political powers that be, both within and outside of government, to educate the public concerning the importance of planning requires persistent effort by some concerned organization over a considerable period of time, or a series of crises or catastrophes that set the need for forethought indelibly in mind. Most influential governmental decision makers do not acknowledge to themselves or to their constituents the crucial relationship between planning and the condition and prospects of people. They are not interested in creating public awareness of this relationship, nor in taking action on severe societal problems until they become so serious and conspicuous that lip service is no longer enough. It is only then that it is in the self-interest of political leaders to support planning to the extent necessary to avoid a breakdown of governmental activity or responsibility that threatens their credibility and above all their reelection.

In democratic societies planning must be supported or at least accepted by the electorate. Governments have ample opportunities in connection with their many activities to create public awareness of the importance of planning. Organizations, groups, and individuals can call the attention of people to a particular plan, provided it is treated in some way and for a long enough time by the mass media of communication. Support of a plan by the mass media is usually enough to secure public approval. Until people are made aware of planning, its effectiveness in democratic societies is limited; most people will not recognize on their own its importance to them and insist that their political leaders make greater use of it.

WILLINGNESS TO ACT

While awareness of the importance of planning is a necessary first step in increasing its effectiveness, people also must be willing to act to resolve the critical needs of their society as well as pursue their individual objectives. As indicated previously, the rights of individuals have been emphasized in the United States almost to the exclusion of the rights of the society to ensure its continuation and advancement as the collective entity on which the survival of its individual members depends. Predominant focus on the interests of the individual and the here and now smothers acceptance of social realities and leads, for example, to the prevailing unwillingness today to accept any increase in taxes or any reduction in present benefits to restore fiscal balance. One consequence is passing on to forthcoming generations a growing mountain of debt that will lower average living standards and heighten social stresses. With few exceptions, young adults are unwilling to even consider volunteering for community activities or a year of national service with the individual benefiting from the experience and society from the productive results of the collective effort. Most Americans acknowledge the need for installations serving the public at large: prisons, rehabilitation facilities, nursing homes, waste disposal sites, power plants. Although they can be incorporated in a community with minimum adverse effects on surrounding property, people near a proposed location insist that the facility should not be located "in my back yard" but anywhere else. A third or more of the eligible population in the United States does not exercise the most basic right and responsibility to vote in public elections, on initiatives and referendums, and other matters decided by the ballot box. Regard for the law is giving way to whatever we can "get away with," and many people excuse what is clearly unethical with specious arguments of legitimacy.

Material possessions are regarded by many people as a better measure of individual worth than qualities of character.

The weakening of societal awareness and a sense of individual and collective responsibility in the United States is not the case in all societies. Some embody the ethical values and social concerns of a dominant religion or a prevailing moral belief. Some have a political history of societal concern and action. All recognize that certain operations are too crucial to their functioning and survival to depend on market mechanisms or a consensus of private self-interests: such as the national monetary, financial, and basic communication systems; military defense; tax collection; public protection of persons and property; postal service; and certain social service systems. Some nations consider that the interests of people are best served by the nationalization of production and many societal activities. Some may contract out some services without relinquishing sovereign control. None share the American expectation that the economics of supply and demand operating through minimally constrained market mechanisms will in time resolve such societal problems as poverty, inadequate low-income housing, or inequitable educational opportunity and health care.

The belief persists in the United States that the fewer the activities of the federal government the better, that the individual concerns of the people collectively will necessarily operate to the benefit of the society as a whole, that they represent in the aggregate the ultimate market mechanism for determining what is best for the nation's advancement and survival. This determination will be made in time to avoid desperate conditions, socioeconomic chaos, or political upheaval. It is generally acknowledged, however, by most people when they think about it that market mechanisms cannot produce plans to control, for example, widespread damage to the environment, drug and alcohol addiction, terrorism, and above all nuclear, chemical, and biological war. The key question is which societal operations and problems are best addressed by sovereign governments with the national effort that they alone can mobilize. And can governments that bear the ultimate responsibility for the welfare of their populations be induced to operate as effectively as successful private enterprises?

SCIENCE, PLANNING, AND UNSCIENTIFIC PEOPLE

As demonstrated throughout history, if plans are formulated and effectuated, progress can almost always be made toward resolving problems and attaining desired objectives. Today, the remarkable advances of science make possible many activities that were beyond imagination not long ago. This poses a basic difficulty for society discussed by C. P. Snow in his book *The Two Cultures*, published more than twenty years ago. The ability of a few outstanding scientists and engineers to advance science and technology and of people generally to make use of these advancements for their own purposes far exceeds their collective capability to employ them successfully for societal, political, and governmental activities and objectives. For their part, political leaders are reluctant to commit themselves to long-range plans for fear of fickle public opinion. They are often indecisive for safety's sake. Self-interest and behavioral restrictions relating to reelection and special interests overshadow any active concerns with the common weal.

The accomplishments of science are impressive indeed. Especially during the past century they have transformed human activities, providing new means of transportation, communication, information processing, and industrial production. New materials have been created and new instruments devised. Medicine and pharmacology have progressed dramatically. Engineering has designed and directed the production of new products and processes during the past fifty years that it is said constitute more than one-half of all those existing today. New weapons of war have been developed. Chemistry, physics, and biology have reached new levels of understanding of the fundamental composition and functioning of inanimate matter and animate life. On all scores science appears to be advancing at an increasing rate, with the prospect of shaping the human condition and future to a greater and greater extent.

Science can improve the condition of the millions of impoverished people in overpopulated areas of the world who are suffering from the effects of deforestation, damaging agricultural practices, periodic drought, flood, and sickness. It can provide the means of controlling overpopulation. It is a critical factor in preventing starvation and the threat of famine for many millions of people, and malnourishment and hunger for hundreds of millions more. Scientific research improves agricultural production, medical treatment, and general health conditions. It provides expository means and methods raising the general educational level and occupational skills of people. It assists in training the managerial and professional leaders needed for developing societies to progress. It provides technical knowledge and equipment needed for industrial production.

In the economically and industrially developed nations of the world, the immediate and pervasive impact of science and technology is overwhelming. It is manifest in the increasingly sophisticated societal systems that are the operational means of conducting human activities in peacetime and in war. Every government, business, military service, profession, and occupation is affected by science and technology. More and more of the hands-on occupations in the human workplace are being performed by mechanical substitutes: automatic computer-controlled machines, robot mechanisms, computers, and artificial surrogate intelligence. Fewer and fewer people have the special knowledge and skill required to design, conduct, and maintain the essential operating systems of society employing progressively more advanced technology. And as the populations of countries around the world congregate in cities, they become dependent on relatively few people to supply them with water, food, shelter, and other necessities and amenities of life that not so long ago they would have provided for themselves or done without in the countryside. The world is characterized by a growing and absolute operational dependence of the many on the few.

Human attitudes and basic behavior have changed little if at all during the recent period of remarkable scientific advancement. As noted previously in this book, people in general avoid confronting realities that disturb them. They create comforting illusions to make life happier or more bearable, are prone to emotional overreaction, susceptible to persuasive enticement, and find it difficult to accept rationally derived conclusions and directives and to act in the public interest rather than their personal self-interest. These human characteristics are not compatible with scientific method and established scientific systems. As long as these attributes endure and industrialized societies become technologically more complex, the gap widens between human predilections and attitudes and the social behavior required for scientifically structured societies to function successfully. Plans with scientific and technological objectives will likely be rejected if they are incomprehensible to the public. Even the well-educated and informed person finds it difficult to keep pace with the rapid advances in science and technology.

This disparity between the rates of scientific and human development could lead to societies with their critical functional systems controlled by the small group of individuals who can comprehend and operate them. If they decided to exercise this technological capability to fulfill their own ambition for absolute power or other personal purposes rather than in the public interest, the 1984-type of society envisaged by George Orwell could come about. The means of societal surveillance, communication, information processing, and enforcement exist today. Rather than being imposed dictatorially from above, as has been tried in part by several recent rulers, such a controlled society could result from a gradual, almost imperceptible transfer of control of more and more of its essential functions to the technically knowledgeable. For democratic societies to avoid this possibility, the body politic must generally comprehend and participate in planning the use of science and technology in society.

CAPABILITY TO PLAN

Humans have demonstrated throughout history—and continue to demonstrate today—their ability to discover, invent, plan, and complete a vast variety of projects and activities ranging from the primitive sled to the supersonic aircraft, the war club to the laser-guided missile, the abacus to the superspeed computer, from the mammoth monuments built by Egyptian Pharaohs more than 4,000 years ago to landing on the moon. History also has shown the inability of most humans to accept and deal with realities, contain prejudice and hate, settle differences peaceably, avoid war, prevent overpopulation, reduce poverty, improve public health, and insist on wise, strong, and humane leaders committed to the public interest. There is no question of man's ability to plan effectively. The unanswered question is whether man can plan successfully at the topmost directive level to advance human society and ensure its survival. There has been some progress in planning to control the industrial effluents causing acid rain and warming of the atmosphere.

Prevention of War

The outstanding illustration of man's inability to cope with the most critical human problems is his failure to prevent war. Means and methods exist that could accomplish this most important of human objectives, but the will to plan and effectuate prevention does not. At least six nations today possess or are capable of producing nuclear weapons in the near future. As many or more can engage in chemical or biological war. It took Roman armies and naval fleets a century and a quarter to eliminate Carthage as a city state in one of history's most implacable hostilities. In Europe at the end of the first quarter of the sixteenth century, there began 150 years of almost uninterrupted religious wars. National and ethnic hostilities have not abated. Today, a combined nuclear, chemical, and biological assault could erase a nation and its population without the means of defense in a few weeks, if not days. With equal military might they could of course annihilate each other. At the present time there is no way of preventing the proliferation of these most destructive weapons which represent man's worst historical legacy.

Nuclear explosives have been greatly reduced in size from their original dimensions without proportionate reduction in explosive power, and made easier to transport and conceal. The raw materials for nuclear explosives proliferate as nuclear power plants multiply and production methods are improved. Chemical and biological agents for military use are easier to acquire as closely related pesticides, insecticides, and other toxic commercial products are manufactured and infectious agents are explored as part of medical research and general scientific inquiry.

Many nations sell armaments, weapons systems, and materials used for military purposes to make the large profits available from these transactions. They actively promote the sale of weapons when they have a vested or potential political, strategic, economic, or military operational interest in the recipient nation. Some countries help others to build plants capable of producing chemical and biological weapons. Most train the foreign nationals to use the weapons systems they have sold them. Some continue to act as advisors. The billions of dollars involved in these provisions produce significant income for half a dozen or more nations. They are reluctant to forego this income and accept the accompanying reduction in employment, especially if the military orders will be filled by another nation—possibly a potential adversary or competitor in the global or regional disposition of military might. Furthermore, if the military weapons are soon to be replaced by the seller, the money from the sale of outmoded weapons can be used for development, testing, and deployment of more advanced and deadly replacements. There are always some individuals and organizations in a nation willing and able to circumvent any legal prohibitions, for profit, a personal cause, or a foreign loyalty.

The technical advancement and spread of the means and methods of extensive physical destruction and societal disruption have added a new dimension to the actions of political adventurers, rebellious groups, fanatical organizations and individuals, and the mentally disturbed. Nuclear explosives can be transported easily and left to explode at some predetermined date. The same can be done with chemical and biological agents. Water supplies can be contaminated or poisoned by remote control. Infectious diseases and plagues can be transported by many means difficult or impossible to detect. Noxious, dehabilitating, or fatal chemical, bacteriological, and nerve gases can be placed in missile warheads, artillery shells, and mines—or released at will from pressurized containers.

Around the world terrorist acts, which have occurred throughout history, are increasing in number, destructiveness, violence, and loss of human life. Drug cartels have all but paralyzed the normal functioning of one nation: murdering judges, law officers, prominent politicians, police, and soldiers and killing and terrorizing ordinary people. A rebel group recently capped some seventy years of terrorist acts by attempting a mortar attack on the official residence of a chief of state. And some years ago a single terrorist act destroyed an international airliner with more than 500 people on board. The daily newspapers report terrorist acts or violence occurring continually in some part of the world.

The situation depicted in the preceding paragraphs is alarming. To prevent world and regional wars and reduce localized armed conflict is the supreme challenge confronting humanity. "At stake in these areas are life-and-death issues far more complex and emotionally charged than the largely symbolic and ideological issues that were at the heart of the long proxy war fought between the United States and the Soviet Union."[1] At few times in history has peace prevailed. The chariot, crossbow, machine gun, chemical weapons, and nuclear explosives were each regarded when first introduced in battle as so devastating that war was no longer a feasible way of settling differences. The same belief is held today by some people that nuclear explosives, nerve gas, infectious agents, and worse weapons yet to come will not be used, and their employment all together at the same time will not occur.

The technical means of preventing war exist, provided several critical preconditions are met. Sufficient people throughout the world must be convinced that the human and environmental destructiveness of war can no longer be tolerated, that military expenditures are better applied to civilian needs, and that war is not an inevitable element of human existence. Hostilities between nations are seldom those of ordinary people on their own volition. They emanate from the political powers that be and government bureaucracies. Political leadership in different countries must be induced to collectively seek to prevent war and to abandon military threat or action as a means of achieving societal goals and any personal political advantages or economic benefits resulting from military advocacy or activities. A number of pre-eminent nations must plan and act together to monitor collateral disarmament and at the same time restrain any nation or group from accumulating military forces and equipment and deploying them with hostile intentions. The people responsible must be able to put aside political reluctance, wishful thinking, and accept the reality of hostile intentions and be willing to act accordingly.

Remote Sensing

Together with other intelligence, aerial reconnaissance can monitor disarmament and a build-up of military might. During and since World War II, aircraft and satellite surveillance of the earth has improved in quality and quantity. Electromagnetic remote sensing now includes photography producing pictures as seen with the human eye and as false-color infrared images recording heat; electronic scanning recording a number of different wavelengths of radiation; and radar images portraying the reflection of pulses directed at ground surfaces. The different values of black to white and different colors comprising these images can be reconstituted by computer manipulation to bring out certain features of detail, and otherwise disclose the very large quantity of information contained in the images.

The sensitivity of remote sensing instruments and the quantity and variety of information that can be derived in this way is remarkable. Pictorial remote sensing portrays many more features on the ground than are shown on maps that are derived nowadays by aerial photogrammetry. The skilled interpreter can identify extensive information concerning land uses and activities on the ground, and with the aid of stereoscopic viewing of aerial photographs observe the relative heights of different features above ground and different elevations of the terrain. Inventories can be taken from the air of rural and urban land uses, field crops, deciduous and coniferous trees, or animals exposed to view from above. A count of farmhouses and single-family detached urban houses multiplied by the average family size provides a closely accurate count of the population in these areas. Certain diseases attacking plants and trees can be detected by remote sensing before they are revealed on the ground. The thin film of oil on the surface of the ocean exuded by fish not far below can be detected, revealing their presence and location to commercial fishermen. Underground archaeological ruins undetected by farmers tilling the land for years may be shown in remote sensing by minute differences in elevation at the surface above or by differences in the chemistry of the soil on top of the remnant walls of structures several feet below the ground surface. The track of a person walking across a lawn to pick up the morning newspaper from the driveway is shown in aerial photography; the blades of grass crushed by footsteps record differently than those upright and undisturbed. These few examples suggest the range of perception possible with remote sensing.

> A satellite image containing literally billions of pieces of information can be converted into a representation . . . that can easily be analyzed by even a personal computer. . . . Farmers should be able to use a home computer to study a satellite image for information on crops and water runoff in their fields. Drug agents could look for fields of poppies and coca without needing expensive computers. Cities could better analyze local land-use patterns and monitor the spread of pollution.[2]

Remote sensing can be conducted from several hundred miles in the air or several hundred feet above ground. With "folded optics," objects the size of a baseball can be detected photographically from a satellite circling the earth 150 miles in the air at 17,000 miles per hour, or "parked" in a geosynchronous or "stationary" position with its speed matching that of the revolving earth below. In pictures taken by "stereostrip" cameras in aircraft travelling at high speed several hundred feet above the ground, the movement of the film through the camera is synchronized with the speed of the plane to produce sharp images revealing small details on the ground. Significant advances have been made in recent years in the quality of remote sensing at night. This is particularly important in military surveillance, since cloud cover obscures part of the earth's surface 70 percent of the time and the movement of troops and military supplies undertaken at night cannot be detected by the unaided human eye.

Electromagnetic sensing of a different kind has been highly developed since World War II. Techniques are available to monitor microwave, radio, and telephonic communications transmitted in the earth's atmosphere from detectors on the ground or in geosynchronous satellites 22,300 miles above the equator. Not only can communications be picked up and recorded, but the detectors can be programmed to note certain key words among the enormous number of communications transmitted continuously. These suggest that the message in which they occur has to do with a subject, organization, person, object, or idea of special interest to those concerned and should therefore be recorded for their immediate reaction or subsequent study. Such selective procedures are required because recording all communications would be unnecessary, impractical, and prohibitively expensive. Monitoring communications is reported in newspapers and journals as the primary purpose and activity of the U.S. National Security Agency during the forty-five years since World War II.

With the means and methods of visual and auditory remote sensing, together with other sources of intelligence, it is possible to identify and monitor installations, facilities, research centers, communications, physical movements, and transactions involved in the production and use of weapons and military materials. Preparations for war can be detected. Concentrations of troops and equipment are difficult or impossible to conceal or camouflage from the alert eyes and keen ears of advanced instrumentation. Activities that suggest hostile intentions or could be developed into military forces or weapons can be detected by a combination of the two basic methods of remote surveillance, and other intelligence existing and still to be discovered.

Aerial Reconnaissance

Such surveillance has in fact been operating since the United States launched its first photo reconnaissance satellite more than thirty years ago. A single such orbiting vehicle can monitor 42,000 intelligence targets of many kinds. The United States now operates five reconnaissance satellites of different types in space at all times. These are accompanied by fifteen additional surveillance satellites launched by the Soviet Union, China, France, and Israel. They will be joined within ten years by satellites belonging to India, Japan, and Saudi Arabia and a fourth one jointly operated by France, Italy and Spain. The scourge of war could be greatly reduced or eliminated if countries would share surveillance information in the common cause of identifying warlike intentions, and if one or more nations or the United Nations maintains a military police force sufficient to prevent any country from actively preparing for war and attacking another country. From both technical and managerial viewpoints such a system can be planned and put in place.[3]

LEADERSHIP

The escalation of local hostilities into regional wars and global conflict killing hundreds of thousands or millions of people and devastating large areas of the world can be prevented. Similarly, planning procedures and technical means are available or can be developed within the existing state of the relevant arts to reduce the severity of the major societal problems of the world. In most cases their severity and in some instances their very existence is the result of inaction or destructive action by humankind. We disregard or are not concerned about disturbing facts and situations we would like to ignore. We are unable or unwilling to acknowledge, confront, and act to resolve the fundamental problems of society or to meet many basic needs until they produce crisis conditions. As a consequence, the resolution of basic societal problems is correspondingly more difficult and costly in human and material resources, or it may be too late for constructive remedy. All too often our political leaders are reluctant to face unpleasant realities and are motivated in their own self-interest to counsel delay or to pay lip service to severe societal problems but refuse to act to resolve them.

Other animal species have developed a system of collective "management" that acts continuously in the best interests of the societal group, responding to changing conditions so as to optimize its functioning and survival. Similarly, it is the political leadership in human societies that is most accountable for operational failures—by inadequate or mistaken actions, by not acting, or by preventing others from acting constructively. As previously noted, the human animal can plan and complete projects and systems of all sorts and sizes. This is most clearly and ironically demonstrated in man's development and application of new technology to progressively more destructive weapons of war during the 10,000 years of civilization.[4] Military planning of course has the advantage over civil planning of more clear-cut objectives and a chain of command that makes implementation relatively free of controversy and active challenge. In civil society the attitudes and behavior of people in general and of their leadership make planning for the best interest of the public at large difficult and often impossible.

People today must act consciously on their own volition to effect changes required by internal developments within their society, or by external developments within the natural environment. We cannot depend on evolutionary forces to effect change or to motivate us to make the needed changes ourselves. We resist recognizing and accepting realities that are emotionally upsetting. For most of us there are enough exacting realities in everyday personal and family life. We avoid the depressive effects of being continually alert to the societal problems we face, some of which we only partly understand. We also can generate a protective screen of favorable illusion to make life more enjoyable or bearable. These traits of avoidance in the population at large magnify the determinative role and power of our political leaders. We abrogate more and more of our self-determination to them as society becomes more complex and difficult.

To the extent possible, politicians also avoid tackling difficult problems not only because it is easier and more pleasant, but more importantly because taking a stand might jeopardize their reelection and careers if their constituents approve of their position at the time of decision but change their minds later on. Any position on an issue can be misunderstood by the public or deliberately misinterpreted by the political opposition. For example, the vote in the U.S. Senate on the use of military force against Iraq in 1991 was almost equally divided between those approving military intervention at any time, and those advocating continuation of the United Nations embargo until it was clear whether it would achieve its objective of forcing Iraq to withdraw from Kuwait without military action. Many people misunderstood the "no" vote favoring relying on the embargo for a longer period as a vote against military intervention at any time, which it was not. This misinterpretation was employed repeatedly by those favoring immediate military action in an attempt to politically discredit those who favored relying on the embargo for a longer period of time. Had the Desert Storm war lasted longer with heavy casualties, public opinion concerning preferable action in the Persian Gulf could have been different. In today's political scene and with today's ethics, a commitment or a vote by political leaders on almost anything can be misconstrued inadvertently or deliberately by the opposition.

Improving political performance in the United States requires fundamental changes. The selection of candidates for public office, the election and reelection of legislators, cannot continue to depend on campaign funds provided by special interests. Public officials must be paid enough to eliminate the need to supplement salary with extracurricular earnings. They could then apply themselves to their primary responsibility of resolving problems and developing opportunities.

This is one of the changes required to encourage the most capable people to run for instead of from political office. They would not spend most of their time, energy, and ability campaigning for office. They would not concentrate almost exclusively on responding to the current preferences of constituents ant the immediate desires of special interests. They would be able to analyze situations thoroughly and act in the collective longer-range best interest of the electorate and society at large. They would be able to maintain their personal integrity and function effectively within prevailing political practices.

Political performance can be improved by reforming legislative procedures, which have become so cumbersome and distorted that producing legislative results has become more difficult, often impossible. The proliferation of committees, subcommittees, and special committees confuses, delays, or derails action. Amendments, riders, hidden changes, points of order, parliamentary procedural disputes, and the filibuster are used for purely political or personal purposes. Legislatures operate as systems of adversarial politics, as if partisan political purposes produce the best outcome for people and society. In some halls of government, adversarial deadlock has necessitated the appointment of special outside commissions to consider issues that must be decided and reach conclusions that are binding on the legislators who cannot reach a conclusion themselves.

Personal and political power is the main motivating force for legislators. The position fulfills the human drive for personal power, prestige, peer and public recognition, the perquisites of public office, almost guaranteed permanent employment, and financial security in retirement. Rather than public service for a time as it was for our founding fathers, politics has become a lifetime occupation or profession. Politicians profess that the self-centered, disinterested, and fickle behavior of the electorate—and the need for large campaign funds—prevent their putting the public interest first. They must "make a living" for themselves and their families. And for most of them, politics or making use of political connections is the only as well as the preferred way of making a living.

It is a combination of the attitudes and behavior of the individual citizen, the electorate, the public at large, and their leaders that determines the conduct of human affairs and the condition and prospects of society. As noted in several connections in this book, the capability to plan successfully exists and is applied continually at all levels of activity—except where it is most crucial for optimum operation and advancement of society: at the political apex of governments.

The mass media of communication will play a critical role in whether badly needed improvements in governance are achieved. Without their persistent support and advocacy, it is unlikely that the electorate will become more informed and concerned and require superior performance by government. And present political leaders will resist change that would require much more of them, and make their position less secure because tenure will depend on enlightened performance.

Public awareness of serious societal problems and public willingness to act cannot be achieved without positive leadership. Demand for superior leadership will not spring spontaneously in the minds of people who are preoccupied with the trials and tribulations of everyday life. Nonhuman animal societies have a genetically established hierarchy of primary procreators, most powerful members, matriarchs, or other forms of superior leadership or pre-eminence. The attitude, behavior, and actions of these primary members are critical for the successful functioning of the societal group and its survival. Activities by these leaders that do not favor the collective best interest of the group simply do not occur.

This has not been the case in human societies since primitive man became civilized man. There is no instinctual or conscious mechanism in individual humans that ensures that their leaders are the most capable people in the society or that the desires of the population as a whole and its leaders are in concert. They are usually different. There are always exceptions, but people in general have rather elemental expectations or ambitions: a means of making a living that provides the necessities of life and some of its recreational pleasures for the individual and family, freedom to worship and circulate, hope of betterment for themselves and their children, security from arbitrary authority and hostile attack. Normally political leaders have additional desires: power and prestige with its perquisites, a higher standard of living with more material possessions and pleasures than most people, and the assurance that they can maintain their position with its privileges. Very few leaders jeopardize these advantages in favor of the public interest. Elected officials usually put re-election above all else. A commonality of purpose and priorities between political leaders and the people they represent is rare in the United States today. This growing disparity between the needs and desires of the public at large and those of its political leaders is a major obstacle to resolving primary problems.

The world population consists of 5.5 billion people at different stages of economic, social, and cultural development—with different levels of literacy and formal education, religious beliefs, customs, traditions, and laws. To achieve worldwide awareness of the problems that must be addressed and the realization that much can be accomplished to resolve or at least mitigate them requires an intensive informational effort by the mass media of communication of the most populous nations. Such a program would have to be initiated by the leadership of these nations, motivated to act to this informational purpose and to respond to the resultant reactions of the people. Can the public be informed in this way and stimulated to insist on constructive action by its leadership? Will the leadership decide or can it be induced to encourage this public awareness and response that might threaten the political position of some individuals?

BUREAUCRACY

Closely coupled with leaders in civil government, business, and the military services are their personal staffs and the much larger number of administrative people they direct or command who provide operational support. Leaders of all kinds are associated with bureaucracies from which they often have emerged into prominence and which they subsequently direct to their own ends, to the benefit of those of the organization or political party with which they are affiliated, or sometimes to the benefit of the society as a whole. Staff support and operational organizations have existed in some form since people first combined into groups acting together.

Bureaucracies enable large groups of people to function effectively by regularizing operations to ensure consistent actions at any given time and over time. This prevents precipitous acts that could disrupt ongoing operations by making sure there is enough time to carefully evaluate proposed changes and, if they are found desirable and feasible, to incorporate them gradually into the existing system. Management anomalies are avoided and mistakes minimized by the procedural stability built into the system, but coincidentally initiative, innovation, and rapid adjustment to new developments are unlikely. Bureaucratic organizations are essential in government, business, the military services, and any other large-scale activity. They are slower acting than some other forms of organization, but they are not inherently or necessarily inefficient.

> The size, form, functions, and efficiency of bureaucracies reflect the culture, customs, and economy of the society they serve. They are also shaped by those who established them initially, and by those whose decisions affect their operations subsequently. Large bureaucracies tend to develop over time an inertia strong enough to effectively determine their own form and functioning. In economically developed countries, they also acquire a procedural or professional competence which increases the usual reluctance to challenge and change the existing bureaucratic system.[5]

Bureaucracies tend to grow without any official policy or statement calling for expansion. Most managers, administrators, and supervisors seek the higher salary or pay and enhanced personal prestige within the organization and in the home that comes with directing a larger group of people. The attitude engendered by private enterprise is optimistic and opportunistic favoring growth and expansion; increasing production or expanding service requires more people. In societies that guarantee full employment, bureaucratic growth accompanies population growth; a place must be found or created somewhere for every new eligible worker. As bureaucracies grow in response to such tendencies, they acquire a momentum of continued enlargement until some external economic or political development curtails expansion or causes a temporary reduction in size. All animal societies appear to have a built-in momentum of growth that favors survival, within limits established by environmental and other natural forces.

Bureaucracies also tend to require more and more paperwork for procedural, operational, or regulatory purposes. As time passes, these requirements escalate into a blizzard of mandatory reports, statements, justifications, confirmations, and other information—much of it not needed. In time, informational and reportive requirements become an intolerable burden on those affected: taking more and more time, requiring additional employees to process the paperwork, increasing costs, reducing efficiency, diverting the attention and reducing the motivation of individuals and organizations from their primary purpose. It has caused many professional people and smaller organizations to cease or modify their operations. Continuous monitoring and firm restrictive controls are required to avoid this characteristic of bureaucracies to produce excessive paperwork.

Some bureaucracies serve purely political purposes. In business and the military services as well as in government, oversize bureaucracies may be the result of competition among executives for greater recognition, rewards, and prospects for promotion within the organization. It is the heads of the larger components of an organization who most often move up the management ladder to the top. The larger the bureaucracy and the stronger the political reasons for its existence, the more likely poor performance will exist and persist until failure to perform requires a temporary curtailment of growth and some improvement in efficiency. Government bureaucracies are not normally motivated to produce the quantity, quality, and technologically advanced products and services needed over an extended period of time for a society to function successfully in today's world of competitive socioeconomic interconnections. If some force does not invigorate the bureaucratic apparatus, the society becomes socioeconomically closed, isolated from the internal and external competition that promotes efficiency and constructive response to environmental and societal developments which in turn necessitate change. A dramatic example of this inherent defect in oversize, inefficient, and overcentralized governmental bureaucracies is their failure in the seven communist countries of the Warsaw Pact in the early 1990s after thirty-five years of autocratic effort to make them work and endure.

Planning and bureaucracy interrelate in several ways. Civilized man created bureaucracy as a way of organizing collective efforts larger and more complicated than those of his primitive forebears. Innate evolutionary forces could no longer effectively direct human activities. People must consciously organize and plan in order to function individually and collectively—for the most part successfully to attain desired objectives, but also destructively when mistakes are made in planning or hostilities are its purpose or consequence. Each society develops a combination of governmental and entrepreneurial organizations. Ideally, this would include "institutions, both public and private, that are largely autonomous within their missions, competitive with each other, dynamic in their adjustment to social needs, and free to innovate."[6]

Unfortunately, bureaucracy presents ever-present difficulties for planning. Besides the built-in momentum to become oversized noted above, bureaucracies tend to be static rather than dynamic in their attitudes and actions, to favor personal security and sameness rather than energy and initiative, the status quo rather than progressive change. This presents a problem for planning because it seeks continual improvement in the attainment of desired objectives. These retrogressive tendencies also exist in business and military bureaucracies, but they are most evident in civil government where there are none of the competitive economic pressures that exist in the business world, nor the complete record of individual performance maintained in the military services. Civil bureaucracies do not function in the longer-range interests of a society when socialized full employment, lifetime job and social security regardless of performance, or purely political purposes are paramount. For a time they may fulfill one of these objectives, but eventually internal developments, scientific and technological advances, environmental events, or global economic competition requires changes that an entrenched, unresponsive, and inefficient bureaucracy cannot effect. This syndrome of civil governmental inadequacy results in part from the human traits and behavior discussed in Chapter 2.

In the United States, the Postal Service is the largest single employer with 760,000 unionized employees, who are among the world's best-paid semiskilled workers, averaging $42,000 a year. It is the eighth largest U.S. corporation in terms of revenues, with annual expenditures of $48 billion in 1990. In most countries, governmental bureaucracies are oversized, to the extent that some of them are a serious drain on the economy and general welfare of the nation. The modern military establishment—including those enrolled in the armed forces, supportive civilian employees, and people working for firms producing military weapons, facilities, and materials—constitute a very large bureaucracy, in the United States several times the size of the Postal Service.

> In civilian industry [the] broad and visible tendency to bureaucratic and corporate self-service is only a smaller shadow of its much larger manifestation in the field of military organization and production. Here there is a truly massive escape from public purpose as the business enterprise becomes part of a vastly larger bureaucratic and political complex.[7]

Governmental bureaucracies do not have to be much larger than needed. Nor are they innately inefficient. They can perform as effectively as nongovernmental organizations that are well managed. To accomplish this in the United States requires several fundamental changes in our political system and prevailing public attitudes. Political leaders should not allow operational bureaucracies to become oversized and inefficient in order to provide the political advantage of an organizational block of votes supporting a particular individual or group of people. Political ambition should not be so consuming that "anything goes" that is necessary to be elected or appointed and reelected or reappointed. Political constituents should not demand that their governmental representatives vote and act at all times in accordance with current "public opinion." This encourages political participation by a group of potential political leaders who avoid public office because they want to be able to act contrary to current opinion and the prevailing desires of the electorate when they believe that this is in the best interests of their constituency, the public at large, or the nation.

It may be that this is more than our society can accomplish as it is presently constituted and motivated. It is still true that governmental inefficiency is not tolerated when it disrupts actions and activities considered essential by the electorate at large or by powerful constituencies. For example, protracted delay in the issuance of social security checks would produce irresistible pressure by the large and politically powerful block of senior citizens to correct this inefficiency immediately. If an approving agency of government responds so slowly to requests for permission to proceed that return of the money spent on developing the product or service and expected profits are threatened, political pressures are brought to bear by the business or industry involved to expedite bureaucratic response. Breakdown of the U.S. national banking system or of governmental "protection of persons and property" would not be tolerated by the public at large.

But more and more of the needs and desires of most people are avoided by our political leaders. As discussed elsewhere in this book they avoid personal commitments, difficult decisions, and actions in the public interest that could threaten their political future. As a consequence, a host of critical societal needs remain unresolved, more because of lack of political will than bureaucratic inefficiency. Examples include clear-cut policies and programs of action relating to energy use, health care, educational deficiencies, drug and alcohol addiction, indigent care, hunger, nuclear and toxic waste disposal, affordable housing, lengthening delays in the legal system, and an increasing prison population proportionately larger than in any other country in the world. The expressed preferences of the majority of people may be ignored in favor of a politically powerful minority or special interest. We appear to be at the critical point where governmental response and action in an increasingly complex and sensitively interrelated world requires political leadership and bureaucratic competence to cope with the worsening problems of human society.

From the viewpoint of administrative management and planning, there are various ways of preventing bureaucracies from becoming so inefficient and dysfunctional that they become institutional burdens on society. First in order, of course, is preventing unwarranted growth by carefully determining if additional personnel are necessary to provide the projected quantity and desired quality of the product or service. Operational responsibilities can be decentralized throughout the organization—as profit centers in business and performance centers in the military services and civil government—where individual accountability is assigned and performance evaluated. This assignment precludes automatic promotion based on longevity and guaranteed employment until retirement. Objective criteria and human judgment can relate managerial advancement and remuneration with performance. One such method is "management by objectives." "The different units of the enterprise determine their own intended achievements during the forthcoming year or over a longer period of time . . . in accord with the policies and objectives of the enterprise as a whole, [which] represent more than a minimum achievement."[8] Contracting out some of an institution's activities provides an indication of comparative efficiency. If the contract agency produces a better product or service at the same or less cost, the contracting institution should be reorganized to perform as well, or it should be eliminated and its activities conducted by another organization. Objective evaluation can be attained by an outside observer measuring performance by the quantity or quality of output, widespread use, customer satisfaction, the judgment of peers, or other means.

Institutional morale and individual motivation are strengthened by a combination of personal and professional experiences conducted or sponsored by the bureaucracy: internal substantive discussions and seminars, formal adult education, attendance and participation at professional meetings. Credits and certificates awarded for such participation are recorded in the person's file and referred to publicly on appropriate occasions. Perquisites can be associated with commendable performance as a formal recognition and as a motivation for continued effort. Formal evaluation of the bureaucratic organization and criticism of specific actions can be encouraged as a means of preventing administrative stagnation and stimulating improvement. If constructively motivated and not malicious or self-serving, "whistle-blowing" should be accepted, respected, and rewarded.

Adoption of such policies and actions to restrict bureaucratic growth and improve performance requires elimination of any conflicting civil service regulations while retaining protection against arbitrary political interference. Whether the best available management methods are encouraged or allowed by those who form or direct administrative organizations is the critical determination. Administrative units tend to follow a cycle of overexpansion and subsequent contraction repeated over the years, except governmental bureaucracies maintained for political purposes, which usually remain oversized and become increasingly inefficient.

There are those who advocate reducing the role of government to the minimum, including contracting out to private enterprise as many governmental activities as possible. Economic market mechanisms provide for competition to determine who can best provide goods and services.

They interrelate demand, supply, and price most efficiently. They stimulate constructive competition, better performance, continual improvement, and innovation. They contribute to the growth, development, and survival of a society. It is the civil government, however, that is the primary directive force in human affairs. It determines the overall political, socioeconomic, and legal systems, foreign policy and national defense, public education and services, safety standards, and other societal functions that require the authority of government. Markets invigorate the economy, produce important information concerning the functioning of the society, and shape human behavior with respect to the operations they perform. They cannot, however, produce the general public awareness, the comprehensive view, and the political support required for the formulation and application of planning in the best interest of the society as a whole. This can be accomplished only by enlightened governmental leadership. Far more important than the popular slogan of "minimum government" adopted by some politicians is the objective of "better government" that is motivated in the public interest and employs the best available management techniques.

ENVIRONMENT

Nature both limits certain human activities and presents opportunities for human attainment. If political leaders and governments do not take these forces of nature into account in planning, they are not acting in the immediate and longer-range best interest of society. We are the product of billions of years of incredibly complex, subtle, and intricate evolutionary development of the surrounding universe, the inanimate physical world, and its vegetative, animal, and insect life. Our earth and its outer environment can now be viewed as a whole from vehicles orbiting many miles overhead or on their way into outer space, with its enveloping atmosphere, oceans, and land masses comprising a single global entity. No national or other political boundaries can be seen, nor any human artifact except perhaps the Great Wall of China 1,400 miles in length. Man must exist within the global environment of interacting forces deep inside the earth, at its surface, and within the atmosphere.

These forces are far more impactful than most people realize. They range from cataclysmic collisions between objects from outer space and the earth, terrestrial earthquakes, volcanic eruptions, tsunamis, hurricanes, tornados, floods, and droughts, to molecular adjustments by flora and fauna to minute changes in the local or global environment. "There is between 1 chance in 6,000 and 1 chance in 20,000 of a cataclysmic collision in the next fifty years. . . . The largest near-Earth [meteoroid] we know of is 10 kilometers in diameter [about 6.2 miles]. If a thing like that hit, the explosion would be a billion times bigger than Hiroshima."[9] Hurricanes and tornados can leave wide swathes of destruction. Large tsunamis can damage entire coastlines. Volcanic eruptions and earthquakes can devastate large areas. Fires lit by lightning can destroy forests and fields or renew their natural growth. Droughts can bring famine as well as vegetative devastation. Monsoons bring life-saving rain and destructive floods to millions of people in eastern Asia. Rivers silt up, meander, or change their course. Erosion steadily washes away and ultimately deposits fertile topsoil in the oceans. At an almost infinitely smaller scale, mutational change in a single element of a genetic code can alter the subsequent development of a species. A microscopic infectious substance can bring disease, sickness, or death to entire animal populations.

Besides being affected by the many forces of nature, human beings have developed in less than a century—an infinitesimal moment in evolutionary time—the power to devastate large geographical areas with nuclear explosions, deadly radiation, chemical contamination, and biological infestation—applied separately or all together, all at once or over a protracted period of time. With modern machines we can destroy or eliminate many natural resources: clear-cutting large forests in a few months or years, strip mining large areas without restoring the terrain, moving vast quantities of earth to make way for human activities and installations, or extracting all known oil within a tiny fraction of the millions of years it took for it to be created by geological processes. We can easily pollute the land, water, and air to the point that our health and welfare are degraded or our survival is threatened. Human activities can impair or destroy the ecological balance of unique environments such as wetlands, coral reefs, and rain forests. We can endanger or eliminate entire species of animals and vegetative life. We are beginning to genetically alter organisms and will manipulate many more in this way in the future including our own species, with unpredictable consequences for humankind and the environment. Our industrial operations may change prevailing weather patterns and regional and global climates.

There are those who believe that science and technology will be able to neutralize or compensate for environmental damages caused by humans and overcome environmental conditions restricting human activities and achievements, thereby assuring a successful future for Homo sapiens. In this scenario, solar or fusion energy will provide unlimited power, freeing people from dependence on fossil fuels which cannot be renewed and will all be gone in time. Conservation will reduce the demand for energy. New materials will be produced to replace the insatiable demand for firewood, lumber, paper, cardboard, and other products, which has depleted natural forests around the world. Improved strains of existing food crops, new species of genetically created edible plants, and synthetic foods will be developed to feed a growing human population. Substitutes will be found for the aerosols and other industrial emanations that pollute the air, deplete the protective ozone layer, and raise the earth's temperature by the greenhouse effect of reflected heat. Storage places and methods of handling highly radioactive nuclear waste with a half-life of several hundred years will be found that do not threaten human, other animal, and plant life directly by inadvertent exposure or indirectly by contaminating aquifers. Toxic waste will be neutralized and the enormous quantities of industrial and household waste will be treated or recycled to prevent any degradation of the environment, hazard to human health, or excessive use of land for storage sites. New pharmaceuticals will provide progressively greater protection against sickness and disease transmitted in the environment. Medicine will continue its dramatic advances in diagnosis, prevention of disease, prosthetics, organ transplants, mechanical substitutes, and noninvasive surgery. Genetic manipulation will reduce abnormalities and gradually produce healthier human beings more resistant to sickness and disease.

New management methods and means of operational analysis will be developed that will extend people's capability to act effectively and constructively as groups or collectively as a society. Robots and automatic machines will perform tasks that are physically dangerous for people, stressful, or psychologically numbing. Surrogate intelligence will direct many routine operations and procedures, enabling people to concentrate on those aspects of an activity that require human creativity, evaluation, judgment, and decision. People will have more time for educational, cultural, and public service endeavors or for increased leisure and recreation. Greater knowledge will permit more accurate forecasting of the weather, earthquakes, and other natural disasters. Incipient hurricane conditions may be defused by cloud-seeding or some other atmospheric intervention. Communication will be so universal and immediate that almost everyone can be alert to current and forthcoming events, with ready access to an enormous accumulation of numerical data, substantive information, and recorded experience maintained at computerized reference centers.

This "brave new world" is possible but a long way off. While a few parts of it are in the process of realization, others depend on further development. More than half the world's population must attain the level of education and understanding required for the projected advancements to be achieved in a democratically rather than autocratically directed world. There must be a common global language or a means of automatic translation that permits intercommunication among people speaking and writing in hundreds of different languages and dialects. Diverse and often discordant customs, beliefs, and ingrained reactions must be coordinated or reconciled sufficiently to permit constructive collective action. Most important are the changes in emotional attitudes and behavior noted at the end of this chapter.

Humanity could be decimated or obliterated almost instantly compared with the time it has taken for our evolutionary development: by a catastrophic collision with a massive celestial body; by a mammoth cataclysm set off by unknown forces within the earth; by pestilential calamity that mankind is unable to mitigate; or by failure to control our own actions on the environment that could threaten the survival of our species. Time will tell whether the human intellect is a more certain instrument of survival than the superior physical size and strength of the dinosaurs compared with other animals was for them in their time of dominance long ago. Our best strategy is to minimize our destructive impact on our environment by ceasing to decimate natural resources for short-term income but long-range economic and ecologic loss. Rather than disregarding or challenging the forces of nature, by taking them into consideration and using them to our mutual advantage we can formulate plans more likely to benefit our longer-range future.

THE MASS MEDIA AND SOCIETY

A look at events occurring around the world today raises the question whether the human species can conduct its societal affairs constructively for its collective betterment and survival. Are there inherent characteristics that limit people's capability to resolve crucial problems by deliberate thought and action, to function cohesively as groups for considerable periods of time? Are there attributes that lead to societal conflict, deterioration, and ultimate self-destruction? Do scientific and technological advances improve societal capabilities or reduce them at least for a time because the rational management they require does not keep pace? Is the genetic instinctive system that causes other animals to act cooperatively to their collective benefit a form of communication and cohesion no longer effective for civilized man? Are the mass media an equivalent form of communication for civilized society today, essential for its functioning, its planning, its advancement, and its survival? So much so that, as argued in Chapter 4, television has become in fact an active element or branch of government?

The mass media are by far the most powerful communicative force in the United States today. They are the modern analogy of the instinctive communication systems that direct the activities of other animal societies. Their primary purpose and immediate effect is the conscious transfer of information among people; all communication provides information in some form. In industrialized nations most people get most of their current information from television, newspapers, and radio. Of these, television, videotapes, and computer screens are the dominant source of information in the United States. "The majority—three quarters of viewers—say the first source they turn to when a major news event has occurred is television."[10] In time, the cathode-ray tube and electronic screen will be the principal means of communicating information throughout the world. Direct sensory reaction to our surroundings, personal observation, and thoughtful study are the sources for a decreasing proportion of the information the average person absorbs.

The main media of communication today include newspapers, periodic publications, books, radio, television, and computer systems in written, graphical, and numerical form on paper, tape, disk, and computer memory. To attempt to treat all of these individually and collectively is beyond the scope and intent of this book. Discussion is limited to television since it is the primary source of information for most people in industrialized countries today and is likely to increase its widespread impact even further as television sets are improved, their cost reduced, and the medium solicited by more organizations, special interests, and individuals for many different purposes.

Effects

Television is so pervasive and powerful in the United States that it is changing the political process, affecting the conduct of government and business, and directly or indirectly shaping the attitudes and behavior of individuals. As television broadcasts multiply in other countries and television sets are available to almost everyone, the medium will become the predominant source of information for the entire world with far-reaching effects on every aspect of human endeavor.

Forty years ago only 10 percent of households in the United States had a television set. Today, almost every dwelling has at least one TV within the home, or available nearby. They are being promoted for installation in various establishments and vehicles for advertising, news, entertainment, or internal security. Network broadcasts include programs and special presentations of many kinds. Entertainment, which constitutes most of network time, includes live performances, movies, animated cartoons, athletic events, quiz shows, and a variety of programs specifically prepared for presentation on television. Advertising, schedule announcements, and program acknowledgments take up from 10 to over 20 percent of television time, involving billions of dollars annually and making many TV stations into what some people call "money machines." Cable TV provides special fare ranging from all news all the time, live and rebroadcast legislative sessions and other governmental activities to sports, musical events, and religious services. The availability of videotapes of television programs further extends the impact of the medium. "[Video Cassette Recording] owners are buying more tapes. Now that 70% of households have VCRs, the so-called sell-through market is the fastest-growing segment of the video business."[11] The competition for viewers, superior audience rating, and maximum advertising revenue is fierce and unrelenting.

The effects of TV are widespread. "Soap operas" shape the attitude toward family and marital behavior and the sartorial and household taste of millions of regular viewers intrigued by the events unfolding day after day on the TV screen. "Quiz shows" entertain a block of viewers with carefully staged contests matching the incidental knowledge of various contestants, with the winners receiving prizes or promotional gifts. "Talk shows" cover a wide variety of miscellaneous personalities, situations, issues, events, oddities—whatever holds the attention of a loyal group of television viewers. Professional sports attract millions to watch their favorite sports and teams. Televising college athletics has transformed them into media events bringing substantial income to prominent universities with winning records. A new classification of semiprofessional student athlete has been created, primarily if not totally concerned with athletic prowess rather than educational achievement. New forms of athletic competition are being devised for television that are a form of nonlethal gladiatorial combat; there is currently a TV program entitled "American Gladiators." Television exposure is essential for most political positions from president of the United States to local officials—to attain and maintain a public and political image assuring voter recognition, for campaign statements and debates, and for announcements and proclamations by officeholders and office seekers directed to the body politic.

Television in the United States is a commercial enterprise, shaped for the most part to optimize private profits within the restrictions and guidelines established by the Federal Communication Commission. The extent to which money and profits are the dominant force is indicated by the recent proposal of the federal government to "auction the airwaves."

> Under law, licenses for everything from broadcasting television to taxi dispatching systems are assigned free to private interests. License holders may then sell their rights at any time, pocketing millions—sometimes billions—of dollars. The [administration] is proposing to end one giveaway by auctioning as-yet-unassigned frequencies, or some of those reserved for government agencies to the highest bidders, the way Washington sells mineral rights on Federal lands. . . . Critics of the plan worry that there are too many risks when the government sells and potentially severs its right to control what has been public property. One fear, for example, is that broadcasters might use what were once publicly controlled airwaves to unduly influence public policy.[12]

Television is not conceived or organized as the main stem of a public information system serving the collective best interest of the society and nation. The constant battle for the highest audience rating reinforces its primary purpose of promoting sales for advertisers by providing entertainment, and directs its programming toward whatever will capture the most viewers' attention regardless of corollary consequences. Advertising revenue is the determinative force for commercial TV in the United States.

Competition for viewer attention pushes television programs toward ever-greater expressive extremes. Some observers maintain that the presentation of extreme behavior informs us of the abnormal realities of some people's lives and enables us to release latent emotions sublimated by civilization. The critical question is whether the regular broadcast of behavioral extremes benefits individuals or society. Do they exemplify and release, or do they favor and incite?

It is their long-lasting effects on the young that are most important. Do they establish in the minds and feelings of children severely distorted and exaggerated images of most people and their behavior? Compared with adolescence and maturity, childhood is the most impressionable period in life. Children have the most receptive hearts and minds, fewer emotional defenses. They are susceptible to suggestion and deceit because they find it more difficult than adults to separate fact from fiction. They have little concept of societal interaction and responsibility. These qualities magnify the impact of television for them.

> Children are struggling to come to terms not only with the disquieting views of the world that come to them through the [television] screen, but with the question of why those in charge of such programs put so many violent images on the air.[13]

Adolescence is the second most impressionable period of life: a time of emotional doubt or confusion, of identification with role models, strong reactions and excitement, developing sexuality, and an awareness of relative strength and social situation. It is the young in each generation who become the adult population of the next. How their early years are conditioned shapes the future.

The Federal Communications Commission recognizes the desirability of TV programs for children and requires that a portion of network television time is devoted to them. Their impact on young viewers increases as more such programs are scheduled. "It has taken a long time for advertisers to wake up to the fact that kids are the adults of tomorrow. ... Capturing a young consumer and keeping him loyal sets a course for predictable sales growth."[14] Children in the United States influence $60 billion of family purchases and an additional $6.2 billion of personal spending. Besides the many millions of advertising dollars spent on networks and syndicated programs, a network of 125 stations covering 122 markets was established in 1989 to reach children aged 2 to 11 as "a way for independent stations throughout the country to make more money."

Clearly, the influence of television on children will become increasingly important for the nation's future.

Television influences the reactions, attitudes, and actions of all its viewers. "In the industry's first comprehensive study of public-service campaigns, researchers have found that television commercials can induce striking changes in people's behavior regarding health."[15] Were this not the case, businesses, political parties, other institutions, and individuals would be wasting billions of dollars on their present use of television. If brief commercials influence people significantly, regular programs lasting up to an hour or many hours as a special series have a profound and lasting impact. With so many millions of viewers, they reach and affect people around the world. Inherent in this widespread impact is a great opportunity to affect human society positively.

All individuals do not respond to television in the same way because they are of different races, historical backgrounds, cultural customs, and economic and educational status. But most people react similarly to broadcast material that evokes fear, hostility, compassion, sensuous desire, and other fundamental feelings and attitudes that they share. This greatly augments the actual and potential impact of the mass media of communication since the common characteristics of people noted in Chapter 2 significantly affect societal activities and planning. We do not like to face unpleasant realities. We are prone to emotional overreaction, prejudice to the point of disregard and cruelty. We look for excuses or scapegoats to assuage our anger or fear. Linked with the desire to avoid disturbing subjects and to shed the cares of everyday life is the wish or the willingness to be entertained. It has been an important element in human life since there has been time for enjoyable diversion. It has been the primary objective of the TV networks in their programming since the beginning of commercial television.

Viewer preferences are not all generated internally in their minds and emotions. What appeals to people can be engendered or encouraged by frequent exposure, by opening up new satisfactions. Television broadcasting can create preferences as well as serve current predilections. It can magnify the appeal of a subject, organization, or individual by frequent and favorable exposure. Conversely, it can depreciate them in the public eye by emphasizing the negative or ignoring them completely. The way an event or a scene is photographed can affect whether viewer reaction is favorable or unfavorable. When shown repeatedly in various connections a single close-up of an individual—displaying a particular facial expression or some other bodily feature—can implant an impression concerning the person's character that may be distorted or untrue. Subject and character assassination or deification are possible on TV. It can communicate instantly to hundreds of thousands or many millions of people facts, impressions, and attitudes. It can deliberately motivate, stimulate,

activate, accentuate, elucidate, elevate, and exacerbate. It also can produce opposite or negative responses to each of these effects.

Content

Since there are only twenty-four hours in a day, an initial choice must
be made among programs devoted to different forms of entertainment,
news, politics, the sciences, and other subjects. Aside from their substantive content, how often different subjects are portrayed affects their
relative importance in the minds of TV viewers. A further choice must
be made within each subject area, field of knowledge, or type of activity.
Which of the vast array of current events, which aspect of the physical
or social sciences, or which of the enormous and ever-increasing inventory
of movies, videotapes, broadcast reruns, and other entertainment materials is selected for broadcast? These choices decide which subjects and
what specific information millions of people see on television, absorb,
and incorporate in their feelings and thoughts. This is an awesome power
and responsibility.

> Over a period of time, the decisions made in network newsrooms can dra-
> matically alter the political attitudes of the nation, limit its attention span,
> trivialize its political debate and diminish its capacity to create a genuine
> long-range political agenda.[16]

Except for the Public Broadcasting System, the content of television
in the United States is determined by the profit to be derived from the
sale of broadcast time to advertisers, other organizations, and individuals,
subject to the constraints and requirements imposed by the Federal Communications Commission and political reaction that could affect the status
of the TV station or the network. As a consequence, entertainment has
predominated in whatever form attracts the most viewers and the largest
profits or comparable rewards: movies, soap operas, quiz shows, news,
sports, animated cartoons, or special programs and series. As noted in
the previous section, the fierce competition among TV stations for the
highest audience ratings leads inevitably to more and more content that
appeals to our suppressed fears, aggressiveness, likes and dislikes, prejudices, inclination to violence, sexuality, fantasies, and illusions.

> When racial tensions are so close to the surface and when fears of crime
> are so volatile, people tend to jump for stories that confirm what they already
> believe . . . it not only taps into expectations, but sometimes it also mobilizes
> deep feelings that people are not aware of. The story is not only plausible,
> in some ways it is satisfying.[17]

Such feelings rooted in our past create internalized attitudes that favor unrestrained emotional reaction to external events, rather than the more thoughtful response of civilized society in accord with the behavioral norms that have developed to enable people to function effectively in the modern world, so vastly different from what existed only several thousand years ago. Emotionally supercharged programs are conceived, produced, broadcast, and rebroadcast on the networks with "ever higher levels of ever more realistic violence . . . with soaring body counts, scenes of people blown to bits, bludgeoned, crushed into oblivion . . . riddled with bullets, beheaded or hammered to death."[18] Not to mention immorality, cruelty, adultery, and sex just short of actual intercourse. Foreplay and copulation are now available on teletapes produced commercially and by ordinary couples willing or anxious to expose their sexual prowess and practices.

Anyone watching network television day after day and night after night does not need a stopwatch to confirm that more and more gunplay, murder, violence, cruelty, horror, criminal behavior, rape, and explicit sex are incorporated in TV programs, appealing to the instinctual predilections of people that are emotionally titillating but do not support the individual and societal response and behavior that advance civilization. Many human activities are transformed by television into "shows." An example familiar to many television viewers is the interruption of many sports events by the introduction of more and more announcers, assorted commentators, and guests competing with the game and with each other for viewer attention and preference. The original form, timing, or some other aspect of the sport developed over time is discarded in favor of maximizing the presentation of advertising. Most TV programs are interrupted at regular intervals for this purpose. In the recent broadcast of a professional football play-off game, 27 percent of game time and 21 percent of broadcast time were devoted to commercial advertising and promotional schedule announcements.

In its pursuit of "newsworthy" broadcasts, television can be intrusive as well as investigative, willing to invade personal and organizational privacy or reticence. Observe the forest of duplicative microphones thrust into the face of prominent persons or ordinary people answering questions posed by inquiring reporters. When pressure to cut costs mounts, there is an increase in the percentage of program reruns, presentation of material prepared by special interests, and widespread use of news reported by a single organization. The high cost of news coverage abroad has resulted in United States television networks relying on only one or two sources of foreign news.

Power

The power of television has multiplied many times since the invention of the first such electronic instrument less than sixty-five years ago. TV has continually exceeded expectations concerning its role in society and the extent of its impact. It can create majority attitudes. Particular subjects can be emphasized and repeated often enough to dominate public attention, but are quickly forgotten without this attention. Soap operas, movies, and other TV programs influence moral values and individual behavior. Favorable or unfavorable reactions can be engendered to actively support or oppose specific issues and individuals politically, to publicly demonstrate, to boycott, or to harass. False applause, laughter, and other sound effects can be incorporated in broadcasts to simulate audience reactions that did not occur. Sympathy, moral support, and money for causes and individuals can be generated by referring to them on news reports or other programs. Reputations and careers can be made, enhanced, or destroyed by several or even a single TV program. Charismatic individuals of various persuasions can use TV to develop large constituencies and regularly receive large sums of money for their religious, political, or other purposes. Exposure on TV is essential for election to most public offices. It can almost guarantee the success or failure of election and reelection campaigns. Competitive sports can be transformed into entertainment spectacles. Television programs can produce panic. Ways of committing criminal and terrorist acts that are difficult or impossible to detect have been demonstrated on TV screens. Television is addictive for some people and enticing for many. It is the primary source of current information for most people. Videotapes of TV programs are used increasingly for educational purposes by individuals and institutions.

These are some of the effects and situations brought about or intensified by television in the United States. They also are induced by radio broadcasts and newspaper articles, to a much lesser degree, however, because of their smaller audiences and the absence of direct visual impact.

Investigative Disclosure

Besides functioning as the main means of communication among humans, the mass media constitute an essential element in the system of checks and balances required in democracies: exposing illegal, improper, and destructive acts, serious errors, significant events, and gradual developments that weaken or threaten the society. Were they not disclosed by the mass media, transgressions would continue unabated and unnoticed—except for the few people directly concerned—until there were conspicuous repercussions. Some serious misdeeds never would become known to the public. Familiar examples of the watchdog and reportive role of the mass media include the savings and loan "junk bond" scandals of the early 1990s, the Iran-contra affair, widespread industrial fraud in connection with Department of Defense contracts, political and police corruption, and Watergate and the resignation of a president of the United

States. In addition to such nationally publicized transgressions revealed by investigative newspaper reporters, there are many lesser misdemeanors usually disclosed to a newspaper reporter, some published in the paper and broadcast on TV to much larger audiences. "The press plays a unique role as a check on government abuse."[19] "We've always known . . . the Framers [of the U.S. Constitution] knew—that liberty is a fragile thing. A very fragile thing."[20]

Except for regulatory and police agencies, newspapers were the main means of discovering and disclosing major transgressions in society before the advent of television; their findings reported directly to their readers and spread further by radio and word of mouth. Recognizing that mistaken accusations and unfounded allegations can seriously affect or even destroy people's lives, newspapers developed their own view of responsible behavior. A new group of "investigative reporters" emerged, required by their editors to support their stories by sufficient fact to justify the allegation of illegal acts, other improper activities, or gross inefficiency by government, business, or any other institution or individual. However, owners and editors of newspapers and TV stations believe that reporters need not identify critical sources of accusatory information, and this has been generally upheld by the courts. They also oppose stricter libel laws in the United States that would make it easier for a person falsely reported as a malefactor to sue the mass medium publicizing the story; "corrections" usually are relegated to a few sentences on an inside page. Newspapers have failed to report some major malefactions until long after the fact, and disclosures tend to follow prevailing opinion and subjects of current interest. By and large, however, newspapers have fulfilled their responsibility as societal watchdogs of the general public welfare. They have been aided in this endeavor by the interest of most people in the misdeeds of others, particularly those in high places.

Newspapers reach many millions of people but television reaches many more. As the single most important source of information for the public at large in the United States, its handling of alleged illegal and irresponsible acts threatening the society is crucial. These are reported in regular or special news broadcasts, in programs devoted in whole or in part to exposés, and in live or rebroadcast legislative sessions and governmental hearings. Because of the depth and breadth of their impact on millions of viewers and those they influence in turn, TV broadcasts must be accurate and fair. In a matter of minutes falsehoods can be disseminated and take root far and wide, misconceptions can be implanted, careers ruined, personal lives severely disrupted, and mass reactions engendered.

Here is a classic case of disinformation, intelligence pros say. Somebody seems to have concocted a transcript of the interview and circulated it. Like a juicy rumor, one person passed it along to another, who passed it on to another and soon it was "fact" and had to be denied. It is not an uncommon method of propaganda.[21]

Policy and Practice

The present policy directing television operations, established and monitored by the Federal Communications Commission (FCC), presumes that viewer preferences produce the best choice of material to broadcast and superior programs presenting this material. Viewer response—determined by consumer reaction to commercials and other promotion in the competitive market place of supply and demand—is presumed to result in the best use of this most important medium of communication for both the individual and the collective interest of the society as a whole. Within the restrictions and requirements imposed by the FCC, broadcasting whatever attracts and holds the most viewers maximizes profits and optimizes use. This policy has been justified during the formative and developmental phases of television. It has resulted in programs devoted for the most part to different forms of entertainment. Now that television has become a force throughout the land so potentially powerful that it is in fact an element of governance, reexamination of its purpose and operation are in order. How must television function as the main means of communication among humans to serve positive purposes comparable to those attained by genetically established interactions among other animal societies and intuitive reactions among primitive people?

First and foremost, the information disseminated must be accurate. There can be no distortive modification, including overemphasis of its relative importance by repetition. It must present different views of the accuracy of factual material or descriptive reporting when its reliability is questioned in the first instance, and there are different opinions concerning what happened in the second. This must be done so that the different evaluations of the factual material or interpretations of what actually occurred, clarify rather than confuse the matter under consideration. Since the medium is such an influential force in people's lives as individuals and as members of a societal group, inadvertent broadcast of erroneous information should be corrected immediately and deliberate deception identified and denied transmission.

> For years, infomercials—program length commercials that masquerade as entertainment or news shows and are often aired on late night TV—have been regarded as the underside of the advertising business . . . "whose only ability to sell products comes from deceptive claims."[22]

Rumors, speculation, and unsupported allegations should not be aired. They are usually wrong or misleading. Even if they are clearly identified as questionable, they can acquire a false credibility if they are repeated often enough. "We have become terribly dependent upon an instrument of mass communications that feels that the cardinal sin is not so much to be inaccurate as to bore."[23]

To the extent possible, broadcast material must avoid engendering or promoting cruel, intolerant, salacious, or other emotional reactions that degrade the individual in today's world and are potentially destructive for civilized society. Common instinctual reactions among animals have enabled them to act constructively throughout their evolutionary development, but in civilized society intellect and historical knowledge have in large part replaced animal instincts. Information presented continually on TV produces common sensory reactions that shape human behavior far more than the animal instincts that are no longer as determinative in contemporary life as they once were.

As the primary source of public information, television must treat the most crucial elements and critical questions confronting society. To fulfill its function of favoring human survival, it must be sensitive to the human condition and the natural environment. It cannot be a captive instrument or mouthpiece for a government, for business, or for any organization or individual. Nor can it allow one of these to preempt broadcast time and exert an undue influence on programming except for brief periods during critical societal emergencies. Television must take into account more than the marketplace of current viewer preferences. People react intuitively to material relating to such subconscious human drives as survival, procreation, aggression, self-satisfaction, or self-determination. These emotional sensitivities have been established during a great many years of evolutionary development. They manifest themselves in the reaction of television viewers to broadcast material relating to these sensitivities directly or indirectly, casually or emphatically as the case may be. Some material may not be noted consciously but is absorbed emotionally and mentally nonetheless.

All of the mass media of communication in democratic societies share four basic functions: dissemination of information, investigative reporting, presentation of educational material, and entertainment. The media also share a built-in propensity toward two extremes: complete governmental control on the one hand, and unrestrained operations by private organizations on the other. The first results in arbitrary political manipulation and control. The second focuses on viewer reaction, which maximizes profit from advertising and other paid programs presenting special interests. Unrestricted governmental or private ownership induces these operational extremes.

Television has advanced technically and its audience has expanded dramatically in recent years. The society it serves has changed. There is need for a new look at TV. Reexamination of how this most powerful medium of communication is conducted raises many questions. Some of these are posed regularly because the answers determine how TV functions currently. Others involve the many considerations relating to the effects of television on the individual and society.

Does ownership of TV stations by either government or private enterprise make it difficult or impossible for the medium to perform its four basic functions successfully? Does the increasing capability of TV to influence public attitudes, opinion, political choice, and legislation constitute a directive power that government cannot cede to private enterprise without abrogating its political role and public responsibility? Would its organization and operation as a public utility or some other form of quasi-public institution enable it to fulfill its societal responsibilities as the main means of public communication and also produce sufficient return on investment to attract the operational capital needed?

Does competition among TV networks and stations in the United States lead inevitably to the broadcast of more and more programs characterized by the behavioral extremes that many people believe are personally harmful and societally injurious? Is TV time being devoted equally among its four primary purposes? Does accelerating competition for audience ratings mean ever-greater concentration on entertainment supporting advertising, to the point that the reportive accuracy and quality of the presentation of news, sports coverage, and other programs are compromised by making them more entertaining to attract and retain viewers?

There is not enough air time to accommodate all those seeking elective office or running for reelection. All of them know the importance of TV exposure to their aspirations. It usually makes the difference between success and failure. How is the finite air time available allocated? To the highest bidder regardless of the source of the money? There are of course organizations and individuals other than politicians who would like as much TV time as their money can buy to further their particular cause. Should their exposure be determined by the supply of time available on demand measured by money? Criteria for such determinations reflect and affect a society in fundamental ways: the political system as it functions in fact if not also in theory, the power structure of the society, the kind of leaders who emerge, and the confidence of the public in them.

There are many operational considerations that affect the quality of television programs and their impact on and enjoyment by viewers. What is the proper limit to the time taken for advertising and other promotional material? Do frequent interruptions—to the extent of broadcasting an Academy Award–winning movie in two segments several days apart—distract the viewer, affect the substantive content, or otherwise impair or distort the effect of programs? Should the deliberate interjection of promotional material into the reportive or entertainment content of programs be allowed? If subliminal images can indeed be projected and absorbed by viewers without their being aware of it, should this be permitted, in view of the wide range and number of inappropriate or illegal behavioral uses to which they could be put? Techniques have been developed which permit the manipulation of television images: enhancing particular aspects of the picture, altering the actual viewpoint of the camera, constructing artificial images by animation that appear so realistic they are accepted as true representations by the viewer. Events can be altered or constructed by shortening, shifting the emphasis, or changing the sequence in which parts of the action reported occurred. Portrayal of a person or situation that is not typical can be fixed in the mind of TV viewers as truly representative if it is repeated often enough. Favorable or unfavorable reactions of audiences to events or programs on TV can be manufactured by faking or eliminating applause, or by reporting predominantly positive or negative responsive interviews. To what extent should manipulated or manufactured images be allowed on TV?

Television programs have caused panic and disclosed how arson, terrorism and other illegal acts can be committed without fear of detection and apprehension, how explosives and other injurious substances can be made from materials readily available, and how locks can be picked. Should such exposition be so explicit that viewers so inclined can replicate criminal acts? How much physical abuse, cruelty, violence, adultery, perversion, and assorted sexual acts should be portrayed regularly on network programs and in movies broadcast on television to viewers of all ages—without even the concluding indication of their criminality, immorality, or at least the painful consequences for the perpetrator, which was once the rule when behavioral extremes were portrayed.

Television and radio broadcast official governmental reports and directives to the population during emergencies and important public announcements at any time. They are also a way of informing the populace concerning governmental actions that are not included in commercial broadcasts but are of immediate interest to many people. These actions may or may not be reported later in special federal and state publications covering different governmental levels or in local newspapers reporting the actions of local governments and other public authorities. To what extent should television disseminate information that is not a source of advertising revenue?

All of the questions concerning television posed in the preceding paragraphs relate to its role and responsibility as the main means of mass communication among people within societies and for the human species as a whole spread around the globe. We require for our survival and advancement—as do all other animal societies—a communication system that serves essential societal purposes. Widespread dissemination of basic facts, figures, descriptive reports, and explanatory statements concerning current conditions, events, and developments are required to conduct human affairs far more complex than the activities of any other animal group. The nature and precise content of this essential information varies of course with the customs, beliefs, and stage of development of the society. In democracies a free flow of core information is needed for people to interrelate, to function, and to attain the factual cohesion among individuals and organizations that enables them to gradually advance their condition and prospects for the future. It must be reliable to avoid the confusion and discord that result when there is no common informational reference, and treated when necessary to allow for cultural and linguistic difficulties of comprehension among major groups of people. Distortions or monopolization of information by any organization or individual prevents the range of information needed to provide the choice among alternatives required for societal progress in democracies. By contrast, the intent of the mass communication of information in autocratic regimes is to make sure that the populace complies with the directives the supreme authority imposes.

Autocracies cover their mistakes or dictatorial acts by fiat. Democracies rely on the mass media to discover and publicize the misdeeds and mishaps that occur in any society. Without this corrective element democracies would gradually erode into basically incompetent and ultimately autocratic societies. As noted earlier in this chapter, investigative reporting is such a powerful component of democratic societies that it must be exercised with deliberate restraint according to a code of correct behavior to prevent inadvertent or intentional injustice. Rumors, unsupported allegations, and mistaken accusations can injure or destroy individual careers and organizational reputations beyond repair. Careful distinction between investigative freedom and propriety and irresponsible suggestion or allegation is required in democracies if the mass media are to fulfill their role of public disclosure. In autocracies, investigative reporting is anathema since it would call attention to inefficiencies and misdeeds that could ultimately lead to the overthrow of the ruling authority.

As much TV time should be devoted to education as is given to basic information, investigative reporting, and entertainment. Television and videotapes are excellent means of gradually advancing the educational level of the populace to keep pace with the increasing complexity of civilized society, particularly in democracies that depend directly on the understanding and discernment of the electorate. Educational programs can be enjoyable and entertaining as well as instructive. Educational topics are as diverse as human knowledge, ranging from simple subjects important in daily life to esoteric fields of knowledge that can be explained or illustrated in such a way that the public at large can make sound choices on these matters when called upon to do so.

Among the characteristics of people noted in Chapter 2 is the desire to escape from the rigors and disappointments of everyday existence, as participants or spectators in art, music, dance, drama, sports, and other forms of diversion and entertainment. Besides providing personal satisfaction, the different kinds of entertainment are significant elements of human behavior and culture. Entertainment has taken many forms throughout history, from gladiatorial combat and burning at the stake to the most exalted music and magnificent art. Television, which is devoted predominantly to entertainment in the United States, disregards other substantive content essential to societal well-being because it relies on advertising and other special interests for its operating income. Networks select the programs that best serve their purposes. Competition for TV time and viewer impact among special interests leads to greater and greater programmatic extremes affecting the attitudes, values, and behavior of the many millions of regular viewers spending hours every day watching television. Witness the progressively more abnormal, violent, destructive, immoral, and unethical behavior permeating entertainment shown on the television screen. Were advertising agencies and their sponsors able to establish and enforce self-imposed limits, advertising would not appear on the sportswear of prominent athletes, on toilet paper, or on the inside surface of the doors to toilet stalls in public lavatories.

Few people can maintain that television serves the four basic societal needs in the United States today. Most people will agree that determining how TV can best perform its communicative function in modern society is a formidable task. Fundamental considerations are involved. For example, with respect to the individual, there is the right of access to information that is available or attainable and of protection from false reporting and unsupported allegation. With respect to society, there is a right of protection from the disclosure of information that jeopardizes national security, is socially harmful, or is against a paramount public interest. Such considerations are relevant to the extent of violence, immorality, and explicit sex displayed on the television screen, to the coverage of criminal executions and the most dramatic courtroom trials, and to the unrestricted and immediate reporting of military operations in wartime and during battle. What should the camera portray in the best interest of the individual and society as a collective organism?

Present policy presumes that maximization of profit from advertising revenue, as determined in the competitive marketplace, results in the best use of the medium and the best program content. TV time belongs to the few who can afford it. Politics are affected because those seeking public office and those up for reelection who have the largest political campaign funds at their disposal can buy the TV exposure that assures success. The same competitive advantage is available to special interests that can pay the price.

All the questions posed in this chapter concerning television are part of determining its best use and programmatic content. Some people maintain this cannot or should not be achieved by deliberate planning. They believe it must emerge over a period of many years as competitive market forces prescribe. Others are certain that present trends unmodified will lead inevitably to politically undesirable if not destructive consequences for democratic society. Unless a modus operandi is established for government and private enterprise to jointly exercise the power of television to inform, develop attitudes, direct events, and contribute significantly to the advancement of society, the government may be obliged in time to take over complete control of this fourth branch of governance or abrogate its sovereignty.

Production of such an explicit operating statement would be difficult. But a special working group or commission, composed of the most capable people representing the principal interests involved, could formulate policies and regulations concerning the ownership, direction, financing, operations, and optimum conduct of television as a primary means of informing, influencing, entertaining, and educating the public at large. In England there is a tradition for such statements or "white papers," each prepared by a special commission appointed by the national government to propose policies and programs on an important issue confronting the nation. After wide distribution and a year or more of discussion throughout the land and modification of the statement, parliamentary action is usually taken.

The present conduct of television in the United States by government and private enterprise represents one set of policies and directives. They have not been combined, expressed clearly, and explained in a single statement. Explicit answers to the questions posed in this chapter are not available to the general public. Either present policies and directives or those proposed by the special working group or commission should be published in a single document, disseminated throughout the country, its contents debated at public hearings, revised as need be, and the officially adopted formulation distributed free to a number of TV viewers—as potential monitors of conformance with the policies and regulations established and sources of suggestions for future improvement.

PLANNING AND HUMAN SURVIVAL

Throughout evolutionary and historical time humans have demonstrated their capability to plan. In different degrees depending on their socioeconomic and cultural development people have collectively acquired the knowledge needed to anticipate and avoid many potential problems, and to mitigate if not always to resolve those that arise. Constructive actions can be taken that produce better results than if no action is taken at all—unless it is decided that no action is the appropriate response in a particular situation. By no means do we always act in our own best

interest. Time will tell whether humans can cope with gradual developments and sudden situations in the future. Catastrophic events could occur
that overwhelm man's capability to plan and act usefully, and he becomes
at least for a time a pawn of nature.

The critical question today and for tomorrow is not whether humans
have the mental ability to plan and shape their future to a degree, if not
to the extent they would like. It is whether their instinctive drives and
emotional reactions and preferences—far older and more basic than mental acuity—will enable people to respond to problems and needs as rationally as effective planning requires. When we look around the world
today, certainly we cannot conclude that we are conducting our societal
affairs successfully. War, insurrection, and armed conflict occur continuously somewhere in the world. Violence and terror have become almost
endemic in human behavior. Poverty is spreading on all continents as the
gap widens between the haves and the have-nots. Over half of India's
850 million people exist below the poverty level.

> In 1969, one in nine persons in Los Angeles [County] lived below the official
> poverty line. By 1987, the proportion was between one in seven and one
> in six persons. That year, one and a third million Angelinos lived in poverty.
> ... The poverty rate also climbed for both the state [of California] and the
> nation.[24]

Starvation decimates or threatens millions of people in the world. Irreplaceable natural resources are being rapidly exhausted: petroleum reserves, rain forests, aquifers, topsoil, and many species of flora and fauna.

At the same time, humans are contaminating the earth with nuclear
radiation, air pollution and potentially destructive warming of the atmosphere, acid rain, oil spills, toxic and household waste, and chemical
pollution of land and surface waters. Fraud and mismanagement are widespread. Executive compensation in many large companies in the United
States has become a matter of personal enrichment at the expense of
stockholders and investors, rather than a true measure of worth and operational performance. The family is threatened as the basic unit of social
stability and child care, with one-half of all marriages in one state ending
in separation or divorce and one-quarter of all households headed by a
single parent. Drug addiction and alcoholism are rampant. Ethical standards are weakened by increasing individualism and materialism.

As if these depressing conditions were not enough, the human species
is unable to adapt its numbers to fit the physical and human environments
within which it must live. People in general retain their primitive reluctance to acknowledge frightening reality, their need to assign supernatural
causes to unexplained events. The need to act collectively in the common
interest is giving way to individual competitive achievement as the standard of behavioral and societal success.

Despite those characteristics of individuals that make planning more difficult, it is not the mass of humanity who are responsible for our present plight and poor prospects for the future. Individuals cannot somehow by themselves combine their personal objectives and self-serving activities into a constructive societal force. Organized joint action and political leadership by government are required. It is people's inability to ensure progressive leadership and attain a system of collective management optimizing individual endeavors and societal actions that underlies the condition of democratic systems today. Civilized society has seen fewer and fewer governmental leaders who are the best people for the positions of political leadership they hold. In the United States, for reasons discussed earlier in this book, many of the most capable individuals of the highest character refuse to consider elective or appointive positions in government. Political representation has become an occupation that all too often requires indeterminate and illusory behavior and compromise of personal integrity to the extent necessary for election and reelection.

Rarely can elected representatives vote their best judgment against current opinion and for that which they believe is in the general public interest. So much money is required for exposure on television and other modes of communication with voters that government officials must cater to the transitory preferences of the electorate, special interests, and individual donors. Television has become the key to the political kingdoms in most of the 39,000 state and local governments in the United States.

> For little known candidates, money has become the currency of viability, valued not only for what it can buy but for what it can symbolize.... "Money is important six to 12 months before an election just to get the media and consultants to take you seriously.... Because of the astronomical cost of television advertising in New York [in 1991] . . . it will take $10 million to win the primary and then defeat [the incumbent U.S. Senator]."[25]

Once elected, the continuing accumulation of campaign funds and the high cost of running for public office guarantee that 95 percent of incumbents will be reelected with only nominal opposition, even after misdemeanors in office are revealed, which are occurring with increasing frequency. Elected officials spend as much time raising money to maintain their image with the electorate and for their forthcoming campaign for reelection as they devote to the duties of the office and the opportunity it offers for political leadership. Any serious analysis of the complex issues involved in governance is relegated to personal staffs, which are growing in number, size, and cost. The capability of the legislative system in the United States to conduct governmental affairs in the general public interest is in jeopardy. Political use of TV is being expanded in some countries: "The imaginative use of privately produced videotapes by politicians and parties is expected to all but obliterate whatever image-making role was left of India's government-controlled television."[26] While private enterprise can provide many public services more efficiently, it cannot perform the legislative responsibilities of government and exercise ultimate political leadership.

Until political systems no longer support oversize bureaucracies, the conduct of government is impaired. Improving normal operations is made more difficult by the lack of motivation for continuous progress, resistance to change, and the tendency toward ever more complicated paperwork, making internal operations more cumbersome and making it more difficult for the public to obtain the services offered. Planning major improvements and projects employing the latest knowledge and techniques is especially difficult, prolonged, and excessively costly when the governmental bureaus that are almost always officially involved in some way are also inefficient. Despite the pronouncements of politicians calling for a reduction in the number of public employees, government bureaucracies continue to grow in size and number.

Projects of all kinds, large and small, monumental and mundane, require plans in some form: a drawing, three-dimensional model, or a conceptualization of the finished product in the minds of those who will produce it. Discoveries in science and technology have vastly expanded man's capability to successfully plan and construct projects of great size and technical complexity: worldwide communication and transportation systems, smaller and more powerful computers, new forms of life by genetic rearrangement, and more sophisticated and devastating weapons of destruction. Intangible products as well as physical objects are realized: new management methods, assembly-line organization, medical treatment, insurance coverage. As would be expected in so fundamental and universal a process, there have been failures as well as successes in planning. But it is clear from their achievements that people can plan and produce impressive accomplishments of all sorts and sizes, simple and complex. There is no reason to doubt that this capability will continue to increase in the future, opening up new opportunities for human achievement.

It is also clear that human societies today are beset with problems so severe that they threaten the well-being or even the survival of the human species. People's ability to plan their activities successfully is not being applied beneficially in the United States by local, state, and federal governments, independent government agencies, and other governmental organizations performing a public function or providing a public service. It is at the top level of governments that the most critical decisions are made in democratic societies affecting the conduct of human affairs within their jurisdictions. It is also where politics reign supreme, determining more than any other consideration the reactions and actions of elected officeholders. Fear of political disapproval prevents elected and appointed gov-

ernment officials from committing themselves or acting decisively, placing
the public above special interests that provide campaign funds, or taking
positive positions concerning plans when there is almost always opposition by at least a minority and the benefits expected will not be realized
until some time in the future. This failure of leadership erodes public
confidence that the democratic political process can conduct societal affairs constructively as well as democratically. Man has the ability to
manage governmental affairs efficiently and to resolve or mitigate societal
problems by planning wisely and well. But the will or willingness to act
effectively to these ends may occur spontaneously in times of crisis, but
is rarely mobilized as part of the continuing operations of enlightened
governance.

Leadership in democracies is of course two-sided. The electorate is as
responsible for the leaders it selects as the leaders should be to work in
the public interest. Throughout history the mass of people have not been
very successful in attaining their modest aspirations: living conditions
sufficient to provide for the current needs of the family, with some hope
of betterment; a peaceful existence without harassment, social conflict,
and war; freedom to procreate, to move about at will, to worship as one
chooses, and to express oneself without fear of retribution. Democracies
have been few and far between. Societal leadership comes about in diverse
ways demonstrated throughout history. Most often it has been royal,
military, religious, autocratic, or dictatorial, with the interest and welfare
of the populace at large taken into account only to the extent it is necessary
to support the self-interests of the rulers or leaders.

Among the social insects, leadership is genetically determined and absolute. Among many animals ritual combat without injury establishes pre-
eminence as leader and chief or sole procreator. In some animal groups,
selection of leaders is by hostile combat; some with many members have
no single leader but act as a unit, following first one then another individual
in no apparent sequence. Communication is the cohesive force that enables all animal societies to function. Without communication leadership
could not be determined in human societies. In industrialized societies
the mass media are the indispensable means of transmitting the information required for them to function, and of achieving and retaining political leadership. Of these television is the most influential today, and
will become overpowering in the future as it links almost everyone in
close or immediate informational contact and functional interconnection.
Because it affects people's reactions, attitudes, judgments, behavior, and
political response with respect to events and issues, television more than
any other single force determines the planning that is undertaken and
realized at the top levels of government. TV affects whether planning is
ignored to the extent possible, whether it is haphazardly applied or carefully formulated, whether it is concerned exclusively with short-range

achievements or includes longer-range objectives relating to basic human welfare and survival of the species, and whether it serves democratic or autocratic purposes.

As a universal process, planning will continue to be an integral part of human affairs, becoming more and more critical as man's activities become more interdependent. Fewer and fewer decisions can be made without organized forethought based on thorough analysis. Fewer and fewer societal problems can be ignored, treated casually, left to somehow resolve themselves, or postponed until public attention and concern are focused on them. The components of civilization are becoming so intricately interconnected that a high order of planning will be required for societies to function. When this is the case, the populace will see to it that political leadership engages in whatever planning is necessary to prevent operational breakdown.

If people around the world are convinced that some effects of their activities severely disrupt the global environment and threaten their welfare and that of their children, they will collaborate in corrective planning if they believe it will relieve the ominous situation. Widespread nuclear contamination or a plague decimating populations around the world could bring such collective action. Unlimited and wasteful use of fresh water by growing populations and the consequent increase in its cost could lead to water conservation plans. Water pollution and soil contamination caused by indiscriminate disposal of sewage, garbage, trash, and toxic waste may require far more effective planning for the disposal of the refuse of civilization than is now conducted. Or when the world's forests have been cut down for the wood or to clear the land for other use without planned replacement of trees, human habits may be changed. In the United States it may become necessary to discontinue the use of hundreds of millions of paper bags and cardboard containers made from wood pulp, discarded after a single or several uses, which must be collected as trash, incinerated, or disposed of in landfills. National and international forest conservation plans or plans to develop a substitute material may be necessary to preserve the remaining forests and woodlands, which contain many species of animal and vegetative life that have not been identified and their potential value for medicinal, agricultural, and other purposes determined.

Emergency plans are drawn by governments and some businesses to direct recovery from the natural catastrophes with which the world is familiar: earthquakes, volcanos, floods, tidal waves, hurricanes, tornados, violent storms. But there may be greater catastrophic events to come: global nuclear war, uncontrollable plague. And judging from geological evidence on the earth's surface, at some time in the future the earth and a meteoroid will collide at a collision speed which could range from 20,000 to 170,000 miles per hour. A small meteoroid would lay waste a large area around the point of impact. A very large meteoroid could so severely devastate the global ecosystem that the best conceivable planning by Homo sapiens would not prevent his becoming an endangered species or even extinct. Unless the collision course of an astral body with the earth is determined some time before impact by astronomical observation and precise calculation, there can be no advance planning for such an unforeseen event. However, if or when it occurs, surviving humans can plan their regional or global recovery.

Answers to the numerous explicit and implicit questions about people and planning posed in this book depend on one's response to the most basic question of all: Can people act rationally to manage their current affairs successfully with sufficient provision for the future to ensure societal advancement and survival?

Human evolution has been characterized by progressive growth in the brain power of the species. The mental capability of its most intelligent and knowledgeable members has increased dramatically during the past 10,000 years of civilization. A store of knowledge has accumulated which will continue to grow and be applied to ever more impressive human achievements.

> Users with little computer skills will soon be able to search through several terabytes of information, or several trillion characters of text, in seconds. The Library of Congress, with 80 million items, contains an estimated 25 terabytes of information. Already, an experimental computer library has linked 150 universities to 40 sources of information ranging from National Institutes of Health data to corporate documents and Shakespeare's plays.[27]

The requisite knowledge and skills exist in human societies to produce a vast array of operating systems, projects, and products. Large cities, scientific agriculture, worldwide transportation and communication networks, and modern military systems could not have been created nor would they continue to function without skillful planning and management. Such accomplishments signify that society collectively and most of its members individually can apply the rational thought required in planning, when motivated to do so by necessity, self-interest, or a particular purpose. It is being done by everybody all the time, in some connection and at least to some minimal degree. There is no reason to suppose that man's individual and collective capability to plan and produce desired results will diminish rather than continue to expand.

Whether man will be able or will elect to act rationally on the controversial political issues and societal problems involved in comprehensive planning crucial for society's future is an open question. Emotional man is far older than rational man. Our earliest ancestors acted on instinct genetically transmitted, finely tuned to favor survival in a challenging and often hostile world. An instinctive awareness and intuitive fear were alert to potential danger. The coitive drive of the male served to perpetuate the species. An innate aggressiveness helped in obtaining food and shelter under threatening physical conditions and competition with other animals. Emotional attachment to other individuals, the family, or larger group increased the chance of survival of the species. Intuitions became conscious emotions in Homo sapiens. Civilization has intensified or brought forth other emotions such as shame, suspicion, romantic love, prejudice, hostility, hate, cruelty, material acquisitiveness, artful deceit, and a desire for immortality. Some of these emotions rooted in the distant past are experienced by those formulating plans and by those affected by them. They may enhance or impair the performance of those preparing the plans and those reacting to them. The satisfaction derived by a few people from their attaining desired results by rational planning is historically a much more recent gratification than the emotional reactions of the many people affected by the planning.

As we survey the world today we see wars, insurrections, overpopulation, widespread poverty and hunger, a growing disparity between the haves and the have-nots, drug and alcoholic addiction, crime and cruelty, unethical behavior, and environmental degradation. There is no comprehensive planning under way that might in time reduce the frightening list of destructive conditions. Rational planning is avoided by politicians in the United States because present circumstances make it politically unrewarding and potentially damaging to their personal aspirations and careers. Election and reelection to office has little to do with overall public administrative capability or performance in office. And the electorate is becoming disenchanted with the existing political system to the point that more and more eligible voters are not exercising this most fundamental right. Comprehensive planning that would address the primary problems and needs of a society involves a number of political disadvantages. Hard facts must be accepted and hard choices made. Unpleasant realities cannot be ignored. It is impossible to treat equally all individuals and organizations involved in comprehensive plans and affected by them. The public interest comes before special interests. Available resources must be allocated among existing activities since there are never enough to meet all needs; some must be withheld from current use and applied to longer-range objectives that will not be attained until some time in the future. The planning process is based on thorough analysis and hard-to-reach conclusions that take managerial time and effort away from campaigning and other political activities. These characteristics of comprehensive planning require a high quality of leadership that few politicians are willing to exercise and the electorate does not demand.

Planning will continue as an instinctive directional force in evolution and as a conscious component of human activities. The planning required to produce systems, projects, and products will continue to make possible larger and more complex human achievements. It will become necessary in order for the different levels of government to operate successfully, to institutionalize comprehensive planning and elect competent political leadership if democratic society is not to regress because it cannot cope with developments. There is serious question, however, whether man can handle his emotional self sufficiently to formulate and implement rational planning: for example, to control his innate aggressiveness which can lead to self-destructive conflict, or his egocentrism which can bring about environmental disaster. Is it possible for civilized men and women to subordinate their personal or family concerns to the collective interest of a larger group or the general welfare of the society at large? Can they conduct crucial human affairs rationally and beneficially for society as a whole and its members individually, advancing the positive aspects of civilization? Or are people incapable of planning and acting to alleviate known problems until they produce crisis conditions and are more difficult than ever to resolve? Can the billions of people around the world—so diverse in many of their emotional reactions to events and issues, their beliefs and motivations, and at such different stages of economic, social, and educational development—collaborate in the coordinative planning necessary to preserve and advance civilization? Does there exist within each of us conflicting emotional and cognitive components of our personality which are a consequence of our acquiring intelligence? If so, will this cause us to overreact emotionally to our societal disadvantage at critical times, threatening our capability to plan and act wisely? Do human societies have genetically built-in difficulties in attaining a high order of democratic leadership that do not exist in other animal societies?

One projection into the future seems certain. Communication will play as decisive a role in the development of human society as it does in the functioning of other animal species. How the mass media in the United States and throughout the world perform will determine in large part what kind of human society develops, the extent and nature of comprehensive planning, and the prospects for Homo sapiens.

REFERENCES

1. Barnet, Richard J., "The Uses of Force," *New Yorker*, 29 April 1991, p. 85.
2. Science Watch, "Satellite Data Adapted for Everyday Users," *New York Times*, 12 March 1991, p. B10 Z.
3. Richelson, Jeffrey T., "The Future of Space Reconnaissance," *Scientific American*, January 1991, p. 38–44.
4. Creveld, Martin van, *Technology and War:* From 2000 B.C. to the Present (New York: Free Press, 1989).

5. Branch, Melville C., *Planning: Universal Process* (New York: Praeger, 1990), p. 150.
6. Shapiro, Harold T., "Public and Private Education," *Princeton Alumni Weekly*, 3 April 1991, p. 2.
7. Galbraith, John Kenneth, "The Sting of Truth," *Scientific American*, May 1991, p. 136.
8. Branch, Melville C., *Planning: Universal Process*, p. 124.
9. Broad, William J., "There's a 'Doomsday Rock,' But When Will It Strike?," *New York Times*, 18 June 1991, p. Z B5.
10. Brown, Merrill, *How Americans Watch TV: A Nation of Grazers* (New York: CC Publishing, 1989), p. 82.
11. Graham, Ellen, "Looking Beyond Hit Films, VCR Owners Fast Forward to 'Special Interest' Videos," *Wall Street Journal*, 10 June 1991, p. B1.
12. Passell, Peter, "Administration Seeks Profits in Plan to Auction Airwaves," *New York Times*, 30 May 1991, p. A1 Z.
13. Haves, Dennis, "TV News: Children's Scary Window on New York," *New York Times*, 11 September 1990, p. Z A21.
14. Swanson, Debbi K., "Independents Eye Kids' TV Market," *Outlook Mail*, 10 December 1990, p. A10.
15. Rothenberg, Randall, "Study Shows Power of Public-Service Ads," *New York Times*, 8 April 1991, p. C6 Z.
16. Halberstam, David, "Where's Page 2 in TV News?, Instant Images, Poor Editorial Judgment," *New York Times*, 21 February 1991, p. Z A19.
17. Bahn, Charles, in Peter Applebome, "The Killing Was Real, The Story Was a Lie," *New York Times*, 29 March 1990, p. A10 Z.
18. Bernstein, Richard, " 'American Psycho': Is Going So Far Going Too Far?," *New York Times*, 10 December 1990, p. Z B1.
19. O'Connor, Justice Sandra Day, quoted in Linda Greenhouse, "State Taxes on Cable TV Upheld by Supreme Court," *New York Times*, 17 April 1991, p. Z C1.
20. Brennan, Justice William, quoted in Nat Hentoff, "The Constitutionalist," *New Yorker*, 12 March 1990, p. 70.
21. Seib, Gerald F., "It Is Diplomatic to Say, 'Please Pass the Disinformation,' " *Wall Street Journal*, 5 July 1991, p. A1.
22. Lipman, Joanne, " 'Informercial' Makers Try to Clean Act," *Wall Street Journal*, 4 March 1991, p. 84.
23. Halberstam, David, "Where's Page 2?," p. Z A19.
24. Ong, Paul, "New Poverty Haunts Urban America," *California Planner*, June 1991, pp. 1, 8.
25. Sack, Kevin, "Candidate's Quest: The Cash to Win a Name," *New York Times*, 6 June 1991, p. A1 Z.
26. Crossette, Barbara, "In India, the Star of the Video Is the Candidate," *New York Times*, 30 April 1991, p. Z A5.
27. Markoff, John, "For the PC User, Vast Libraries," *New York Times*, 3 July 1991, p. Z C1.

SELECTED
BIBLIOGRAPHY

Ardrey, Robert. *African Genesis*. New York: Deli, 1963.

Berelson, Bernard. *Human Behavior*. Shorter Edition. New York: Harcourt, Brace, World, 1967.

Branch, Melville C. *City Planning and Aerial Information*. Cambridge, Mass.: Harvard University Press, 1971.

——. *Comprehensive Planning: General Theory and Principles*. Pacific Palisades, Calif. Palisades Publishers, 1983.

——. *Continuous City Planning*. Chicago: American Society of Planning Officials, Planning Advisory Service, Report 290, April 1973.

——. *Planning: Universal Process*. New York: Praeger, 1990.

Brown, Merrill. *How Americans Watch TV: A Nation of Grazers*. New York: CC Publishing, 1989.

Brugioni, Dino A. "October 15—Discovery of Offensive Missiles in Cuba," Chapter 6 in:——————. *Eyeball to Eyeball, The Cuban Missile Crisis*. New York: Random House, 1990, pp. 187–217.

Bullitt, Stimson. *To Be a Politician*. Garden City, N.Y.: Doubleday, 1959.

Cobbett, Steinberg. *TV Facts*. New York: Facts on File, 1985.

Creveld, Martin van. *Technology and War: From 2000 B.C. to the Present*. New York: Free Press, 1989.

Eastman, Tyler, Sydney W. Head, and Lewis Klein. *Broadcasting/Cable Programming, Strategies and Practices*. Belmont, Calif.: Wadsworth, Third Edition, 1989.

Ehrlich, Paul R., and Anne H. Ehrlich. *The Population Explosion*. New York: Simon and Schuster, 1990.

Fagan, Brian M. *The Journey from Eden: The Peopling of the World*. London: Thames and Hudson, 1990.

Goleman, Daniel. "Insights Into Self-Deception." *New York Times Magazine*, 12 May 1985, p. 36.

——. "New View of Unconscious Gives It Expanded Role." *New York Times*, 7 February 1984, pp. Y19, 20.

————. "New Way to Battle Bias: Fight Acts, Not Feelings." *New York Times*, 16 July 1991, p. Z B1.

————. "Perception of Time Emerges as Key Psychological Factor." *New York Times*, 30 December 1986, p. Y16.

Lee, Alfred McClung, and Elizabeth Briant Lee. *The Fine Art of Propaganda: A Study of Father Coughlin's Speeches*. New York: Harcourt, Brace, 1939.

Lichter, S. Robert, Linda S. Lichter, and Stanley Rothman. *Watching America: What Television Tells Us about Our Lives*. New York: Prentice Hall, 1991.

McLuhan, Herbert Marshall. *Understanding Media, The Extensions of Man*. New York: McGraw-Hill, 1965.

Mini Dragons, *Singapore*. New York: Ambrose Video Publishing. 1990.

Ornstein, Robert, and Paul Ehrlich. *New World, New Mind*. New York: Doubleday, 1984.

Padilla, Salvador M., Editor. *Tugwell's Thoughts on Planning*. San Juan: University of Puerto Rico Press, 1975.

Padover, Saul K., Editor. *Thomas Jefferson on Democracy*. New York: New American Library, A Mentor Book, 1939.

Parcenti, Michael. *Make-Believe Media, The Politics of Entertainment*. New York: St. Martin's, 1992.

Richelson, Jeoffry T. *America's Secret Eyes in Space, The U.S. Keyhole Spy Satellite Program*. New York: Harper & Row, 1990.

Ritchen, Fred. *In Our Image: The Coming Revolution in Photography*. New York: Aperture, 1990.

Smith, Hedrick. *The Power Game: How Washington Works*. New York: Random House, 1988.

Tugwell, Rexford G. "Earthbound: The Problem of Planning and Survival." *Antioch Review*, Winter 1949–1950, pp. 476–94.

————. "Notes on the Uses of Exactitude in Politics." *Political Science Quarterly*, March 1939, pp. 15–28.

————. "The Superpolitical." *Journal of Social Philosophy*, January 1940, pp. 97–114.

————. "The Utility of the Future in the Present." *Public Administration Review*, Winter 1948, pp. 49–59.

U.S. National Committee for the Decade for Natural Disaster Reduction, Commission on Geosciences, Environment, and Resources, National Research Council. *A Safer Future: Reducing the Impacts of Natural Disasters*. Washington, D.C.: National Academy Press, 1991.

U.S. News & World Report. "Who Will Control TV?" Special Report, 13 May 1985, pp. 60–68.

Wall Street Journal, "Technology: Taking It Personally." Special Report, 21 October 1991; "Telecommunications: Spanning the Globe." Special Report, 4 October 1991.

Weaver, Kenneth F. "The Search for Our Ancestors." *National Geographic*, November 1985, pp. 561–629.

Wilson, James Q. *Bureaucracy: What Government Agencies Do and Why They Do It*. New York: Basic Books, 1989.

World Commission on Environment and Development. *Our Common Future*. New York: Oxford University, 1987.

INDEX

About the Author

MELVILLE C. BRANCH has been Professor and Distinguished Professor Emeritus of Planning at the School of Urban and Regional Planning
at the University of Southern California, at Los Angeles, since 1966. His
many books include *Regional Planning: Introduction and Explanation*
(Praeger, 1988) and *Planning: Universal Process* (Praeger, 1990).